where's Thena?

I need a poem about...

Insightful and witty
Poems

by Thena Smith
edited by CC Milam

where's Thena?

I need a poem about...

Insightful and witty
Poems

by Thena Smith
edited by CC Milam

BLUE GRASS
publishing
Mayfield, Kentucky

For information write:
Bluegrass Publishing
PO Box 634
Mayfield, KY 42066 USA
service@theultimateword.com
www.theultimateword.com

ISBN: 0-9745339-8-X

1st ed.
Mayfield, KY : Blue Grass Pub., 2004

Cover Design: Todd Jones, Tennessee
LD Hand font and LD PeekABoo font used with permission by
Lettering Delights
Proudly printed in the United States of America

10 9 8 7 6 5 4 3 2 1

Dedication

Lord I write these poems for You
And I lay them at Your feet
Only You can bless my poems
And make my words sound sweet.

Only You can take my words
And turn those words into a phase
That will heal a hurting heart
Or be a sacrament of praise.

From my heart I offer these
As instruments of love to share
That You bless each of those they reach
Is forever my heart felt prayer.

Thena
4/06/04

This book is prayerfully dedicated to God and to the family
and friends that He has sent to bless me. With thanks
and love to hubby Ron, and daughter, Melissa Hamilton. Ron
never once complained during all of those late nights when I
would be up until 2 am working. Melissa was a constant
source of inspiration and encouragement. For once words
fail me in the effort to describe the depth of love I feel
for them. And thanks to my new friends and adopted
sisters, Linda LaTourelle and CC Milam without whom
this book would still only be a dream!

Where is Thena?

There are three little words
That I hear each day
And I go on alert when I hear people say
"Where is Thena?"
It's not that I'm famous
Or ever will be
But with a strange name like mine
Folks tend to remember me.
And they know right away
That a joy of mine
Is to write them a poem
Or rhyme them a rhyme.
So whether I'm at church
Or at my home each day
Or to the supermarket I'm on my way
Or on the telephone
I hear them say
"Where is Thena? I need a poem…"
That it only takes me a minute
To write something inspiring
or something amusing
Can sometimes confound them
And be rather confusing…
"How did you do that"
Is the question they ask
"Who told about this
Or how did you know about that?"
God gave me a talent
On a day long ago
And I promised Him then
That I would let people know.
—Thena ©

About Me...

ABOUT ME

Perhaps you've picked up this little book and you are flipping through it trying to figure out just who in the world this person is and if you should buy this volume. Well, the answer is *YES*, it would make me so happy if you bought it! That would be two sales for sure that I can count on! (I know my friend Shirley Stockel will buy one!)

So, now at least you see that I have a sense of humor and I'm told that is a good thing. I realize that sometimes it is debatable, but in most cases, it is a good positive trait.

If you really want to know about me, I have just recently retired from government service—nothing exciting, just as a personnelist, and now I am having such fun starting what I call "*My Real Life*". If you are nearing retirement age and sometimes get discouraged and over stressed, hang in there because it is certainly worth it!

In February of 2004, I turned 59 and thirty-nine of those years have been spent married to my college (and current) sweetheart. He is a handsome and intelligent man and I am a blessed woman to have found him! And thirty-four of those years have been dedicated to being mother of the world's most wonderful daughter, Melissa. She is not only pretty but is very intelligent just like her dad. I always tell folks when I introduce them that Melissa got her looks and her brains from me, because her dad still has his!

I was born on a small farm in Lowes, Kentucky, moved to Paducah, Ky at age 12 and back to Lowes at 16. After graduation, I headed off to school in Murray, Ky. Hubby and I met and married while attending Murray State University and then we moved on to the University of Missouri. The Navy took us to Arlington, VA where hubby did his active duty and I worked for Army JAG at the Pentagon. Our daughter was born during this time and I "retired" from my federal job in order to stay at home with her. After a number of years in Virginia, hubby was sent to Coronado, CA with his job, and we fell in love with the close-knit village atmosphere. When we got the chance to move here permanently, we did, and now we have been here for over 20 years!

For all of those bosses that I have had down through the years who liked me, encouraged me, urged me to follow my dream, and even nagged me to do it. This book is filled with heartfelt gratitude. Please know that every bit of encouragement, every kind word throughout a person's life is a blessing that is worth its weight in gold.

There are those who ask why I write...should they not just as well ask...why do I breathe? To live and love and think and hurt and not to record it is unthinkable and to me, undoable. I learned to write in first grade and it has been my passion (along with reading) since that age. I entered a poetry contest in third grade and won and my little poem was published in the local paper....I have never gotten over the thrill... and never shall... I was asked by a women's group that I was visiting to share a poem with them and if there was a collection of my work available. From my pocket I produced an envelope, a napkin, a sales receipt and various other scraps of paper, each with verse scribbled on them. "Yes," I told them, "here is a collection of my work and there are many more."

This book has always been my dream and thanks to a wonderful lady, Linda LaTourelle, who is Bluegrass Publishing, it is becoming a reality.

Now, finally, the collection is in a more presentable format. I hope you enjoy and are blessed by it.
...Now go hug someone, will you?   ~Hugs, Thena

My Other Names

During the routine
Of my daily life
Unbesmirched by stress or strife
I was quietly called by my name
And it was always pronounced
Just the same..."Thena"

But if aggravation I had caused
That was a THE..(and then a pause) NA!

And if there was a catastrophe
(like an avalanche or I almost
Burned down the ranch) It was
THENA BLANCHE!!

And when I was in the family's good graces
And the cause for smiles on all the faces
I was known to some
As "sweetie pie" or even "hon".

But when I became my hubby's wife
He called me the "joy of his life"
And when he felt so inclined
I was also "sweetheart of mine".

Then came the name
Unlike any other
I still melt when I hear it....
It's simply ....
......Mother!

Who Is Thena?

I have always known
Without a doubt
Just who I was
And what I was about.

I have known from the onset
Of my life
That my desire was to be
A mother and a wife.

I loved being a child
On the family farm
With handmade quilts
To keep me warm.

But there were things
I always knew
That when I grew up
I wanted to do.

I wanted to marry
A wonderful man
And have a child
To hold my hand.

I wanted to write
The things deep in my heart
And to share God's love
I wanted to do my part.

So I wrote and I wrote
And I began to share
And I realized
That God had answered each prayer.

How to Write A Poem

If you need a poem
And you don't know where to start
Just put your pencil to the page
And write what's in your heart.

The words don't have to rhyme
And maybe they seem odd
But just write what's in your heart
And leave the rest to God.

For if He gives you the nudge to write
To console a hurting friend
Just put your pencil to the page
And the words the Lord will send.

Don't worry about what people think
About your verse or you
For God knows someone who needs
Just that word from you!

?

If you need a poem
And you don't know where to start
Just put your pencil to the page
And write what's in your heart.

TABLE OF CONTENTS

ADOPTION AND BIRTH POEMS

I was not adopted, but my parents impressed upon my tender heart when I was very young, that adopted children were very special. I had a cousin who lived in the "city" who was a bit older and was adopted. Her parents had gone through great difficulty in finalizing the adoption and had another child removed from their arms and returned to the birth mother just before the adoption became final.

Our family spoke of this in hushed tones because everyone felt the heartache of growing to love a child and then having to send him back to his birth mother. Those who had welcomed this little one into heart and home for almost a year now had to adjust to life without him. They missed his little baby laugh, his wobbly first steps and the feel of his chubby little arms around their necks. It was such a difficult time for them that they almost gave up the idea of ever having a child to call their own. But, finally, just when all hope seemed gone, it happened and a baby girl was theirs.

This made such an impression on me that I have always been drawn to both the birth mothers who seek the best for their children and to the adopted parents whose hearts long for a child.

I also feel compassion for the child who searches for their mother and the birth mother who wonders about the baby she gave away.

The Moment We Saw You

We knew the moment that we saw you
That our baby you were meant to be,
That God had brought us together
It was so plain to see!

For there was a bond between us
That stirred my soul inside
I felt such love within my heart
It was if, in joy, my spirit cried.

Your daddy was so happy
I knew he felt it too,
That special certain something
That existed for us with you.

We knew that we already loved you
From the moment our eyes met
And the love planted in our hearts that day
Has not stopped growing yet!

Each day we love you more and more
And so thankfully I confess
That you complete our family
And you are our happiness!

?

I never really thought about it
Before that wonderful night
But now I'm a firm believer...
I believe in love at first sight.

Heart of a Birth Mother

It should have been the best of times
The happiest time in the world
A time for bonding between a mother
And her precious baby girl.

Oh what love poured through my heart
What first I set eyes on you!
How could I provide the life I wanted you
to have
Whatever could I do?

Agony, untold and beyond description
Filled my heart each day
As I made up my mind that my decision
had to be
To give my most beloved babe away.

I gave you up not because I didn't love you
Oh, if only it had been that way!
I gave you up because I loved you more
than life itself
And loved you more each day.

I gave you up because I saw in you
Beauty and intelligence and grace
Because I saw a love of life and desire to live
In your precious baby face.

And live you would and live you must
A life that would be wonderful and sweet.
I knew that I must do what was best
Oh, how my heart did beat!

I've prayed that someday God above
Would bring you back to me
And that the heart that loved you then
and loves you still
You would be able to see.

I pray that someday God will answer that prayer
And let us find each other,
How wonderful will be the reuniting
Of you dear child to this yearning mother!

My heart will never beat so fast
Nor will it ever be so thrilled
To finally have that child shaped spot
Once again recognized and filled!

And I pray that God will let us be dear friends
Which is quite enough for me
If I can once again have you to touch and hold
And love for eternity!

?

Thank you Father for those who care
And whose gifts answer other prayers
As they offer to loving parents
Most precious of all gifts on earth
The child to which they gave birth.

17

Love at First Sight
(Mommy)

The doctors took you from my womb
And placed you in your daddy's arms
He was ready to give his life that very instant
To protect you from all that could harm.

I watched him as he snuggled you
And cuddled you so tightly
I knew in that moment
He would not take fatherhood lightly.

I never really thought about it
Before that wonderful night
But now I'm a firm believer...
I believe in love at first sight.

Love at First Sight
(Daddy)

The doctors took you from your mother's womb
And placed you in my waiting arms
I was ready to give my life that very instant
To protect you from all that could harm.

Oh, how happily I loved and snuggled you
As I cuddled you so tightly
I knew in that moment
Fatherhood was not to be taken lightly.

I never really thought about it
Before that wonderful night
But now I'm a firm believer...
I believe in love at first sight.

Our Miracle

It was a miracle how you came into our lives
As you reached out for a gentle hug
That was only the start
For you reached out to get a hug
And instead you took our hearts!

You were drawn to us in such a special way
That brought tears of joy to our eyes
How delightful and how wonderful
And what a joyous surprise!

You reached out in wonder and love for the world
And as your eyes rested on each new thing
We saw them through your baby eyes
And it was like welcoming the birth of spring.

Oh, God above could not bless us any more
Than He has done for us today
For He has bestowed on us more joy
Than our words could ever say!

And for now and ever more
When we count our blessings here on earth
We will thank the Lord in Heaven
For the precious mother who gave you birth.

?

Oh, God above could not bless us any more
Than He has done for us today...

You Were the Answer to My Prayer

You were the answer to my prayer
You were my dream come true
I asked the Father for a miracle
And He sent me you!

You were the greatest gift
That I could ever crave
I asked God for a precious gift
And you were the gift He gave!

You were the reason that I could smile
You were the words to the songs I sang
I asked God for a tune
And He gave me everything!

He gave me a reason to wake up each day
With a baby to love and games to play!
He gave me a reason to laugh and to smile
Making my life seem more worthwhile!

The days were sweet when you were a baby
And grew sweeter every day
You brought me such joy and happiness
And brought unbounded love my way!

And each night when I count my blessings
I thank the Father above
For answering my yearning hearts deepest prayer
And sending you for me to love!

You were the greatest gift
That I could ever crave...

To My Mom
(Adopted)

You were the answer to a prayer unspoken
By a baby too young to know
That she needed the love of a nurturing mother
To protect her and watch her grow.

You were the greatest gift
That I could ever crave
God knew the innermost needs of my heart
And you were the gift He gave.

You were the reason that I could smile
You were the words to the songs I sang
God gave me the song and the tune...
In you, He gave me everything!

The days of childhood were sweet
And grew sweeter every day
As I grew and I knew such great love from you
And the happiness you brought my way.

And each night when I count my blessings
I thank the Father above
For knowing the cries of a tiny heart
And sending me a Mom such as you to love!

?

As I grew and I knew
Such great love from you...

Because I Love You

Because I love you
I will let you go
And let someone new
Take you into their home.

Because I love you
And want the very best
I will let you have another heart
In which to make your nest.

Because I love you
And feel I might fail to be
The mother that you need
I will let someone else succeed.

I will never forget you
First child of my body and heart
I will cherish you forever
Even though we may be far apart.

And someday when you are old enough
Your birth mother you may want to see
And I will be waiting eagerly to meet you
And a wonderful reunion that will be!

So sweet dreams my little one
I send you off to those whose arms ache
To hold a baby of their own
And in whose hearts you already have found a home.
Because I Love You...

Because I Love You...

Not of Your Flesh

Of your flesh
I may not be a part
Our love was born
From God's very heart.

For God in His wisdom
Knew that we were the pair
That a special bond
Would forever share.

He sent me to you
And forever I'll be
Grateful to God
For my Mom....His Blessing to Me!

Announcement of Adoption...(Boy)

In our hearts he was already our song
God kept our baby secure and safe from harm
Until He could place our little one in our arms.

Our child was waiting for us to find him
For us to find the words to our song
And he was just waiting patiently
For us to come along.

God has a way of bringing together
All things that are meant to be
And the joining of baby and parents
Is a glorious sight to see.

Come and join in our celebration
Sing with us our song of love
For the child so sweetly given us
By the Heavenly Father above.

23

God's Chosen Mom for Me

When I was a baby and so brand new
God gently and lovingly placed me with you.

He answered your prayers for a baby to love
And watched over our family from Heaven above.

In my baby heart I felt so cherished
As my childhood you blessed, watched over and nourished.

Through childhood and teen years never wavering
You were always with me, each moment savoring.

You taught me so much through all of my years
That when I count my blessings my eyes fill with tears.

I will never doubt God's love for me what ever I do
For He loved me enough to send me to YOU.

Happy Blessed Mothers Day to the
Mom God knew I would have chosen!

?

I've Been Adopted!

I've been adopted by the Father
Lord of the Earth
And Heaven above
Secure in His Promises
And surrounded by His Love!

A Family

It was not so long ago
That we did not know you.
And it was not long ago
We had not met.

But suddenly we were together
And our families seem to fit!
Now we are no longer strangers
But families brought together by love.

It does not matter that our time together has been
shorter But rather that our time has now begun
And the two families that were once separate
Are now no longer two but one!

Though we did not know you as an infant
And could not watch your progress as a tiny lad.
We gratefully watch your journey into adulthood
And for this privilege we are very glad!

So in this album are loving memories
Gathered since you came into our world
We treasure each photo in our hearts
Are grateful to God for your very being
And that of our family you are now a part.

?

If ever there were a gift from above,
the greatest gift is our Father's love.
He gave His Son so that we might live.
And with His grace adopted us.
I'm so proud that I am part
of the one true family!

Written by Linda LaTourlle

25

ALBUM DEDICATIONS

Scrappers and Rubber stampers are among the most generous and tenderhearted folks in the universe. I'm convinced of it! Not only will they create albums for themselves, but, at the drop of a hat (or a photo) they will create albums and cards for family, friends, and at times...for strangers!

On various scrapbooking message boards to which I belong, I have witnessed random acts of kindness and compassion to the extreme and I have been the recipient of such. On the Creating Keepsakes Message Board, I was surprised with a wonderful album of pages created by several dear ladies with each one illustrating a poem of mine. I went to an expo in Chicago to meet with dear friends from The I Dream of Scrapbooking Website which was created by a dear friend as a home for some of us who lost our home message board after being on it for over a year together. I have made friends there that I consider family!

And on the PCCrafter Message Board, the ladies surprised me with bundles of wonderful handmade items during a Valentine Swap. On the Two Peas board one of the ladies started a special Thena Club. I had done nothing to deserve this honor and privilege except to be a part of these loving groups. My very first club was the Yahoo Group, Leora's Scrapbooking Clubhouse, and they have done so many wonderful things for me through the years, that I can't even begin to mention them all!

So much of what this book is about, is due to the ladies who are members of the groups listed above. They have encouraged me, cheered me on and dare I say it- even nagged me about writing this book!

So many times I have been asked if I had a poem that a person could use for an introduction or a dedication to an album that I have created several variations along with ones I have used for my own pages. I hope that you will enjoy the little verses that I have chosen to share with my friends.

This is my album
About my life
Before I was a mother
And before I was a wife.

This is the story of who I was
Before I became who I am now
This is the story of who I became
And about the person and became
And when I became me and HOW!

?

Album Dedication

I wanted to give you a special gift
That will be a treasure for years to come
So I created this little album
And it is a very special one!

On each page are places just waiting
For photos and memories and such
A place to place the mementos
That you treasure so much.

I will be happy to help you
Just send the album back to me
And I will do the pages for you
Documenting each special memory!

Not Just An Album

This is not just another album
Not just another book
This is opening up my heart
And giving you a look.

In this album there are pages
To remind me who I am
And of those I love so much
With memories in printed form
That I reach out and touch.

There are pages about the baby me
And pages of the teen
Pages of my older years
And all the years in between.

As you open up the album
And watch my story unfold
I pray that there are years of memories
Not yet recorded and not yet told.

An Album for You

We made this album
Just for you
Full of love
And photos too!

We put it together
With love from the heart
With affection we crafted
Each single part.

For when someone has a friend
As wonderful as you
Only the very best gift
Showing our depth of love will do!

So Glad You're Home

Here is a little gift for you
That you might think incomplete
But I made it just for you
And it's really quite unique.

I want to document the work
You did while you were away
I want you to look back upon
Each very special day.

I put these pages all together
But I am lacking your memories
Once you furnish those to me
This book is sure to please.

Look through your photos
For those that mean so much
And I will help you build this book
A treasure you can hold and touch.

Years from Now (Album)

Years from now as you take a look
At this special little memory book.
I pray that you will be blessed
By all the love and tenderness
Recorded on each and every page
And that your love only improves with age!

Here is a little gift for you...

Your First Album

Here it is, your first album
Straight from your young heart.
Filled to the brim with wonder
Your photos—your art!
This book records how you see
The world around you today
It reflects the awe and wonder
In all you do and say.

Another Family Album for Christmas

Family Christmases are special
And stay in our hearts forever
Every tradition or gathering
Is a wonderful family treasure.

Family from near and far
Traditions and events
Vacations in plush hotels
Or camping out in tents...

All these things are recorded here
With photographs and stories too
A family album just waiting
For me to share with you!

A Gift Album for Dad

I searched and searched for a gift
Which my love for you would impart
When all the while the gift was close at hand
For it was within my heart.
I took the love from this heart of mine
And fond memories of you
And from those came this special gift
Made as only love can do.

Because You Are Special

Because you are special grandmother
I have created from my heart
A very special gift for you
Filled with your grandchildren's art.
Each tiny little picture
Whether in crayon or finger painted smudge
Is placed there with great love
And each one comes with kisses and hugs!

Grandparents Album

I wanted to give you a special gift
That will be a treasure for years to come
So I created this little album
And it is a very special one!

On each page you will find
Created with photos and such
Remembrances of special times
That I know you treasure so much.

Your grandchildren are all accounted for
On pages bright and gay
To bring happiness to your Christmas
And joy for your every day.

You can add to this special album
As you take photos through the year
And keep this booklet to remind you
That we hold you very dear!

I will be happy to help you add to it
Just send the album back to me
And I will do the pages for you
Documenting each special memory!

When God Created You

When God created you
The world was truly blessed
With all the special joys
That make a family happiest!

For you know how to do
The things that warm my heart.
You touched my life with loving care
Right from the very start!

You showed me that you believe in me
And all I'm dreaming of...
When God created you, dear Grandparents,
He blessed my life with love!

I made a little brag book just for you
So that all the world could see
Just how much I love you
And how special you are to me!

Grandparents Are Special

Grandparents are special
Handpicked by God above
To shower blessings on families
And show them His love!
I made a little brag book
For all the world to see
How much I love you
And how special you are to me!

Album Dedication
(Young to Teen)

I wanted to give you a special gift
That will be treasured for years to come
So I created this little album
And it is a very special one!
On each page are special memories
With Photos starting when you were young.
Watching you mature and grow
Has been a pleasure and such fun.

Throughout the years you have always had
A special place in my heart
You were someone extraordinary
And I felt it from the start.
You have become such a lovely young lady
So beautiful through and through
You are such a joy to know
And I am so very proud of you!

To A Wonderful Coach

How do you say thank you
To someone so grand
A leader, a mentor
A wonderful man?

How does one thank you
For all that you've done
To make life so special
For a brother or son?

We can't find the words
To say from our heart
But hope that this album
Will do it in part!

33

ANNIVERSAY

An anniversary is a special date. In this instance, I am thinking of wedding anniversaries and I have included some of my favorite little verses that you might use for cards for your family and friends as well as some verses for use on scrapbook pages for your sweetheart.

My mom and dad were married at Christmas Time and it made their wedding anniversary very easy to remember. Celebrating it amongst the hustle and bustle of the Christmas season posed a real problem, however.

I am entering the era where the anniversaries of our peers are in the 30+ year range and ages in the 60+ range. I am a romantic at heart and I love to write mushy, sentimental poems about my hubby and for other folks to celebrate falling in and remaining in love.

Not too long ago, I attended the 50th anniversary reception for some dear church friends. I tried to keep out of way of their official (daughter) photographer but snapped quite a number of photos.

I created a scrapbook for the couple and took it to them at church the next Sunday. I saw them at a distance exchanging glances that I didn't understand—did they like it, I wondered.

After the service they shared with me that their daughter's camera had been without film during the entire celebration and mine were the only photos they had. They were so appreciative of the photos and the album. And I was thankful that I followed my heart and took those photos. I was also thankful for a digital camera and a computer which allowed me to create quickly and efficiently and share that work with them in such a short time!

For My Sweetheart (Husband, Wife)

We have been together for 50 years,
You've shared my joy
And happiness,
You've shared my sorrow
And tears.

You're like a drink of water
When I've been in a barren land,
You've been my strength
To lift me up
When I've been too tired to stand.

I will always be grateful
And I thank the Father
Each time I kneel to pray
For sending such a
Loving husband (wife)
And precious friend my way!

?

I do not take it lightly
That you trust me with your heart
I will treat it gently
Each and every part.

On Your 50th Anniversary

What was it like
On the day you wed?
What were the things you did?
And what were the vows you said?

What were your thoughts
When you said "I do"?
What were you feeling,
The two of you?
What sweet memories
You must share together
You have lived through sunshine
And stormy weather.

I love the way you are today
And I love the special things you do
You are shinning examples of
A love that has remained true.

So on this Special Anniversary
I pray God to bless
Your day with joy and sunshine,
Love and Happiness!

?

Some must search their whole lives through
To find a love that is pure and true
But we were blessed beyond compare
To find the love that we now share.

36

To My Husband

You are my best friend
The music to my words of praise.
Only my calendar of life
You are my holidays!

You are the husband
That I always hoped I'd find.
You are my sweetheart always
You are my Valentine!

You are the reason for my being
You are the ornaments
On my Christmas tree
I am so blessed beyond all measure
By having you to share your love with me!

Only God Can

Only God can take two people
He's intended for each other
And guide them through the years
Until they discover one another.

Only God can take two people
With their preferences and goals,
Then blend their gifts and talents
And unite their hearts and souls.

Only God can take two people
With the joys they're dreaming of
And make them one in marriage
Through the miracle of love.

Congratulations and Best Wishes!

Renewing My Vows to You

Fifty years ago when we were wed
Sweet and loving vows we said
I promised that my whole life through
To you my love, I would be true.

Years have gone by
And I still feel
That the love we share
Is just as real.

We have shared the good times
As well as the bad
We have celebrated in happy times
And clung together in the sad.

We have become closer each year
Becoming more "us" and "we"
Growing closer every day
And feeling less just "you" or "me."

I have no problem with wondering
Just where I stop and you begin
For 50 years ago I married my soul mate
My sweetheart and my best friend.

And with no hesitation in my heart
I cherish the renewal of my vow to you
To love you and cherish you my love
And spend the rest of my lifetime with you!

I cherish the renewal of my vow to you...

Mom's Anniversary Without Dad

Mom, I celebrate with you today
The wonderful love you had
With the loved one you called husband
And the dear one I called Dad.

I know that it is hard for you
To celebrate this day
Without your sweetheart beside you
Since he was called away.

But know that he is with us
In everything we do
For he lives inside of my heart
And in the heart of you.

So many times I see his face
In the eyesight of my heart
And know that of my very being
He has a noble part.

So celebrate with me today
And I will celebrate with you
The goodness of the Lord above
For the husband He gave you.

Mom, I celebrate with you today
The wonderful love you had...

39

BABIES

What could be more special than a baby! I can't think of anything. Babies have a way of bringing joy into not only the immediate family but also the whole family circle and the neighborhood.

I can still remember the feeling that the world stood still for those first few weeks with a new baby. I knew that life outside my little world was going on but I didn't pay much attention to it.

Babies are wonderful and the sweetest addition on earth to a family!

Here are some verses for baby cards, new moms and dads, new grandparents and those pages that you will be creating to celebrate each of these.

?

The day you arrive
Will be a special day
Engraved in our hearts
In a special loving way!

We will celebrate it every year
And remember it every day
As the most wonderful moment
When God sent a miracle our way!

A First Born Child

A firstborn child were you
And you do those things
The firstborn child
Always will do.

You are reliable and always share
You are so compassionate
And show others every day
Just how much you care.

God creates firstborn's
In such a special way
Knowing the families He chooses
Will be blessed by them each day.

Tears-I'd Pick You

Forgive me if I'm teary
I'm not really sad or blue
It's just a special mommy thing
That all of us Mommies do!

Today my baby looked at me
As we were all snuggled in bed
And placed his hand upon my face
And such sweet things he said!

"If I could pick just one friend
To last my whole life through
I know just who that friend would be
Mommy I'd pick you!!"

A Precious Moment

I watched you today
As you shared a moment,
The two I love most
In the whole wide world—
My husband, love of my life
And our precious baby girl!

I pray that you will always
Have the bond
That you share today
And the joy you share
In each other
Will never fade away.

May your daddy always
Be your hero
For he is my hero too
And each day
We thank our Father
For the precious gift of you!

I watched you today
As you shared a moment,
The two I love most
In the whole wide world—
My husband, love of my life
And our precious baby girl!

God Bless the Mommies

God bless the mommies
And bless the daddies too
Who try to teach their children
To be good and kind and true.

God bless the moms who have to work
And must trust others for a child's care.
When inside their aching hearts
They wish they could be there.

Bless the ones who wish each day
That they could stay at home with each
And love them and cuddle them
To guide them and to teach.

Bless the moms that stay at home
And take the task to heart each day
Of nurturing and guiding children
Teaching them as they work and play.

God bless the mommies who though so tired
And weary at the end of the day
Take time to kneel by a little ones bed
And take the time to pray....
God Bless the mommies.....

?

God Bless the Mommies
And Bless the Daddies too...

Baby Shower Poems and Announcements

Baby Shower

Looking at all the wonderful gifts
Should give anyone's heart a lift!
Knowing that people care so much
Should bring a smile and your heart touch.

People came and celebrated
For the baby who is long awaited.
They brought tokens of their love
For this blessing from above.

And through the years when you have time
Look back at this page and little rhyme
And know that whatever you do
Lots of people care for you!

Baby Announcement

We are so excited
To present our baby to you.
Because Mommy and baby are resting now
Here's our invitation to you:

We know you'd like to meet her
And that is our wish too.
So we've set aside a special day
Especially for you:

DATE:TIME:ETC

~~~~~~

Birth Announcement for Boy

When God sends an angel down to earth
We call this heavenly miracle.... birth.
Our angel is here and we want to share our joy
with all the news of our precious boy!

If Baby Has Not Been Born Yet

Come and Join us
For lots of party fun
To Celebrate the birth
Of my Mommy and Daddy's son!

I will be there with you
(Mommy and me)
But I'll make my real debut
A bit later you will see...

Mommy will take lots of photos
To share with me once I'm born
When she can wrap me in your lovely gifts
To keep me safe and warm.

?

Come and Join us
For lots of party fun
To Celebrate the birth
Of my Mommy and Daddy's son!

You are Invited!

You are invited to a party
Held in honor of mommy and me
I am sorry I can't visit with you
But I've not been born yet, you see.

I'm still nestled in my mommy
Up close to her tender heart
And God will give me a gentle nudge
When my birth journey I should start.

So until I make my appearance
And can visit with you there
I thank you for the baby gifts
That you bring for me to use and wear.

Than you for the goodies
You might bring to me
I can hardly wait to join you
And thank you properly!!
If baby has arrived...

Come and Join us
For lots of party fun
To celebrate the birth
Of my Mommy and Daddy's son!

I will be there with you
As cute as can be
To make my party debut
This is my opportunity.

Thank you for attending
I can hardly wait to meet you
And mommy and I together
Will be there to greet you!!

It's a Celebration!

So glad you came to celebrate
With mommy and daddy and me
I've heard lots about you
And welcome this opportunity.

I know that Mommy loves you
And is happy that you're near
Cause I am with her every day
And all that stuff I hear.

She says that you are all such good friends
That she wanted to share this day
And tell you how blessed she is
That God sent me her way!

Baby Shower Gift

Look at all the outfits
That baby has to wear
Everything from frocks
To tiny underwear!

Look at all the tiny clothes
That will keep my baby dressed
Of all the tiny outfits
Don't know which ones I like the best!

Thank you seems like a tiny phrase
To say for such a lovely day
Of sharing my joy and happiness
For the baby on the way!

Little Prayers
And Blessings

Prayer for Baby's Room

May sweet gentle slumber greet you here
As you rest your little head
And may God's angels watch over you
As you snuggle in your little bed.

May lullabies await you when you're tired
And may your mommy's arms enfold you there
And may your every precious day
Be handled with love and prayer.

Prayer

God bless you and keep you
Safely through the night
And may He wake you gently
When comes the morning light.

May He fill your life with sunshine
And fill your heart with peace
And may your days bring happiness
And joys that will not cease.

God Bless You and Keep You
Safely Through the Night...

Good Night Little One

Good Night, Sweet Dreams
My little sleepyhead
I kiss your cheeks
As I place you in your bed.

You've had such a busy day
So many toys with which to play
So many games of peek a boo
So many things a baby must do.

You kept your mommy smiling today
And daddy could hardly wait to say
"I'm home, where is my little one?"
You blessed our day with so much fun.

So sleep little angel
Gently through this night
And wake us when morning comes
With your coo's of sweet delight!

Bless This Child

Father God in Heaven Above
Look down upon this child you love
And grant her peace throughout this night
And gently awake her with the morning's sweet light.

Let angels their sweet watch keep
Over this loved one as she sleeps
And guard her dreams that they may be
Restful and loving dreams from Thee.

Good Night Sleepyhead

Goodnight my little sleepyhead
I kiss your cheeks and place you in your bed.
You've had such a busy day
With so many toys with which to play,
So many games of peek a boo
And so many things a babe must do.

You kept your mommy
In smiles all day
And daddy could hardly wait to say
"I'm home, where is my little one?"
You blessed our day
With so much fun.

So sleep little one
Gently through this night
And wake us with goo's
And coo's of pure delight.

Baby Album Poems

Look at Me!

Look at me and you will see
That I'm having lots of fun
And life can only get better
'Cause I've just begun!

In this album are the photos
Of me from the very start
Including ones taken at my beginning
When I nestled near Mommy's heart!

On My Way to ONE!

My first six months
I'm pleased to say
Helped me get started
Now I'm on my way...
I'm on my way
To being one
And completing
A whole year of fun!

I'm on my way...
A year has past
And today I find
I'm ONE at last!

Walking Into Two

I hold back sentimental tears
At the most precious view
As my little one year old
Walks out of one and into Two.
One was an adventure
With days that were all too few
Precious little infant days
Gone now that you are two.
I hold back my tears and smile again
For my heart always smiles at you
And I will adjust to the fact
As all moms do---
That my darling is now two!

The Thrill of Three

Look at me
I'm finally three
And I'm as excited
As I can be!

I'm so much smarter
Than I was at two
And there's so much stuff
That I can do!

I can run so fast
And talk like a pro
Oh, there's so many things
That a three year old knows!

I love being older
I love being three
But most of all
I just love being ME!!

Baby Black Eye

Today I had a crash
It happened in my belly
I took a big ole tumble
And hit my baby head!

I banged my eye and head
But that's not the only part
The pain went right through my face,
Into my mommy's heart!

52

Baby's First Wipeout

Today I had a crash
My walker went astray
I lifted up my hand
And zoom it ran away!

I banged my nose and head
But that's not the only part
The pain went right through my skin,
Into my mommy's heart!

Baby Booties

Tiny little booties
So precious and so sweet
How wonderfully soft are they
On my little one's feet...

Human hands made tiny little socks
For the little one I love
But the precious one who wears them
Was made by God above.

Oh God, Thy handiwork
Inspires such awe in me
Especially such a dainty masterpiece
As the child in front of me!

Human hands made tiny little socks
For the little one I love...

Baby Hands

Some day these precious
Girlish hands
Will clutch a bride's bouquet
Will wear a wedding band of gold
Will wipe their own babe's tears away.

Someday these hands
May know of pain and sorrow.
But for today,
I will treasure each moment
And train her for
Whatever will be tomorrow.

Baby Pool

Oh, how cool
To be a baby
In a pool!
I laugh and smile
And thinking all the while
How cool is my pool!

Splish!

Splish! Splash! In the Pool
It's so much fun
To play in the sun
But it's totally cool
To swim in the pool!

In Your Pool

The summer sun
Is smiling on you
As you play in your pool
And every little water droplet
Wants to kiss you too.

Summertime is special
And the fun things we do
But the most special part of summer
Is sharing it with you.

In the Pool

When the first rays of summer
Come bursting through
Splishing and splashing
Is what I want to do!

I put on my suit
And take off my shoes
And the water splashes away
All the winter blues!

I swim in my goggles
And splash with my flipper feet
Summertime is my favorite time
And the pool is my favorite treat!

Splishing and Splashing
Is what I want to do!

You Gotta Look Cool For the Pool!

All the kids in the neighborhood
Come out in the summer looking good!
For in the summer there is a rule
You gotta look cool for the pool!

A goggled face is good summer fare
If it covers up the face and hair.
And it's even better if while there
It gives your neighbor quite a scare.

So find your suit and flipper fins
Snorkel hose and favorite friend
And pull goggles on your suntanned face
And summer fun you can embrace!!

You Gotta Look Cool For the Pool!
(version two)

All the kids in the neighborhood
Come out in the summer looking good!
For in the summer there is a rule
You gotta look cool for the pool!

If you have a lovely bonnet
Put it on and count upon it
To keep your face from getting red
While looking lovely upon your head!

And when you are suitably attired
You can relax and play for it's not hard
To be looking stylish, cute and cool
While playing in your plastic pool!

56

All Wrapped Up!

Peek a Boo little love!
All Wrapped Up,
I see your tiny face
Peeking happily out at me
Lost in soft cottony embrace!

I reach out to touch you
And hug each tiny baby part
As you play peek a boo in the softness
And leave your footprints on my heart!

Big Sis

I am the big sister
And it will be such fun
I'll have a playmate that stays all night
And doesn't leave when day is done!

I have more than enough toys
For the two of us to play
And I have lots of storybooks
For her to read each day.

I have lots of room
In my bed for her to sleep
I will be very quiet when she's napping---
I won't even make a peep!

My Mommy says not to worry
And not to fret or fuss
That she has more than enough love
For the two of us!

Oh, How I Love My Baby Toes!

I can wiggle my toes when I am glad
Scrunch them up when I am sad
And when I'm angry I have found
I can dig my toes into the ground!

I can put my foot up to my nose
And smell each of my baby toes.
I can kick up each little footsie
And count each tiny little tootsie!

I can pull my toes up to my cheek
And into my mouth to taste toes so sweet.
I love my fingers and my nose
But my favorite pastime involves my toes!!

Ten Little Toes

Ten toes to tickle
And ten fingers to clutch
Two little lips to whisper
"Mommy, I love you this much!"

Two little legs to run to me
Two little eyes to light up
Two little arms to hold out to me
And ask "Mommy, lift me up?"

Two little hands to patty cake
Two little ears to hear
All the wonderful things in the world
And one heart to hold them dear!

My favorite pastime involves my toes!!

A Smile is a Joy to See

A smile is such a joy to see
It means so very much to me
But when I hear your laughter burst out
I know that 's what life is all about!

I love the look upon your face
It's like a warm and sweet embrace
I hear you laugh and then I grin
And wait for you to laugh again!

I love the joy that your eyes show
For when you laugh your face has a glow
So laugh and laugh again my dear
For it is music to my ear!

Your New Smile

First you had a toothless smile
To brighten up your face
And it caused Mommy such delight
Shining like a warm embrace!

Then your little pearly teeth
Appear in dainty rows
And when you flashed those pearls at me
I melted to my toes!

And now the day has come
As teen time you heart embraces
When your smile is camouflaged
By metal dental braces.

59

Baby's First Smile

The photographer captured your image
Digitally and on film
All the relatives oh-hed and ahhed
Over the photos done by him!

They said it looked just like you
And wasn't the photographer smart...
But the very first image I have of you
Was captured in my heart.

The moment I first saw you
And looked into your tiny face
A snapshot was permanently implanted
In a very tender place.

A mommy's heart stores precious things
To ponder all life through
And among the treasures hidden there
Is the very first smile from you.

Your Smile

Your smile is so soft and sweet
As it slowly spreads from cheek to cheek.
I understand why I have read
Words that poets oft have said
Speaking of this beauty all the while
Saying that for one glimpse
They would walk a mile.
Lovers spend so much time
Penning verses of romantic rhyme
While mothers write in baby's book
Of such a sweet and precious look!

Babysitter Poems

For more than ten years
Your love you've gently shared
With all of our little ones
Left within your care.
We've blessed the day we found you
And we've thanked the Lord above
For the goodness that surrounds you
And the way you show His love!
Today we honor you
And wish you all the best
Praying that your days be joyful
And that your retirement will be blest!

How Do We Thank You?

What do you say to an angel sent to earth
Who has loved and nurtured your kids?
What do you do to show your appreciation
For the wonderful things she did!
Well, the angel lady is you
And we are sending this card to say
How wonderful we think you are
And send our love your way!

?

We've blessed the day we found you
And we've thanked the Lord above...

For Our Favorite Sitter

Mommy and Daddy call on you
When they want to leave the house
And they know that they can count on you
To keep us quiet as a mouse.

They know the neighbors won't complain
That we have been running wild
Or that you let us get into trouble
Like some undisciplined child.

They know that you will set a time
For us to go to our bed
And that we won't be a problem next morning
From being a terrible sleepy head.

I guess this is a little thank you
And what I'm trying to do
Is to echo my parents thoughts
And say our favorite sitter is YOU!

For a Wonderful Sitter

For years you've nurtured our kids
And you touched the hearts of those you've met.
This little card is to show you
That those who love you don't forget.
Our prayer is that it blesses you
As you look at the names inside.
And know that when we say "Our Sitter—Our Friend"
We say it with love and pride.

Baby's Kissing Spot

Angels bending down to earth
Kissed my darling from her birth
Until on her tiny head she's got
A tiny little kissing spot!

The hair was sweetly worn away
From being kissed day after day.
How precious is that spot to me
A reminder of love that I can see!

And every day since she's been born
I kiss her on that spot so worn
And I thank the Heavenly Father above
For this darling He sent for me to love!

Belly Button

I have a tiny button
In the middle of my belly
When I giggle it makes it wiggle
Like a tiny bowl of Jelly!

?

In the middle of my tummy Is my belly button
Although it doesn't button Anything at all.
I don't understand its need It doesn't give me speed
But it's really kind of cute Fastening up my birthday suit!

63

First Bouquet

Sweet smile upon your little face
Holding hands behind your back
You toddled up to me and then
Your smile turned into the biggest grin.

Hands outstretch to show me
The sweetest gift
That touched my soul and gave
My heart a lift
You offered from your little hand to mine
A precious bouquet.....a dandelion!

For you mommy, you said and then
Turned around to pick a 'lion' again.
Oh, someday you may send me a grand bouquet
But nothing will ever match this day!

God's Blessing...Your Miracle Baby

God always hears our prayers
And would have you to know
That His timing is always perfect
Even if sometimes we think it slow.

He knows the love that you hold
In your tender heart
And of your special caring family
Chose this babe to be a part.

So cherish all of the special things
That life will have in store
Knowing that as much as you love this child
God in Heaven loves you even more!

Lord, Send Us a Child

I look around me each day
And in my arms I see
A great big empty spot
Where a little babe should be.

I know that sometimes
It takes awhile to become
The doting mom and dad
Of a daughter or a son.

But Lord I've waited
(Though sometimes impatiently)
To have the joy of motherhood
So please send a child to me!

I have had tests and labs galore
And have done all that I can do
I know that my hearts desire
Can only be filled by you.

Please send us a baby, Lord,
Someone to love and cherish
To dote upon and love forever
To feed, nurture and to nourish.

I will be forever grateful
And I'm sure that you can see
How much I want a little child
And what a good mom I'll be.

Please send us a baby, Lord, Someone to love and cherish...

Stay With Me

Mommy, come into my room
And rock me in your chair.
If you need to rest a bit
You can do it there...

Mommy could you hold me
As I get comfy in my bed
And you can cuddle just a bit
After my story is read...

And could you call my daddy in
And have him turn out the light
For when he's in my room with me
I don't mind the dark of night...

I hope that you don't mind it
That I need to have you near
For when you are both with me
There's nothing that I fear!

I don't mind the darkest night
Or the strange things in the day
For when your arms are around me
All bad things go away!

Mommy could you hold me
As I get comfy in my bed
And you can cuddle just a bit
After my story is read...

Why God Created Blue

When God created colors
So beautiful and bright
He created lovely hues
For daytime and for night.

He created grass
So lush and green
And browns for earth and
Yellow for spring.

He created pink for little girls
So full of frill and lovely curls
A lovely color, I agree
And fit little girls so perfectly.

But how to define a little boy
Not just any color would do
So God looked around Him at the sky
And decided to create a perfect blue.

For boys, he knew, on a sunny day
On their backs would love to lie
And look up at the awesome sky
To watch the fluffy clouds go by...

And boys would love
To wade in the streams
Splash in brooks, go rafting too
And water reflects the sky so blue.

Boys would scoff at pretty pink
If wrapped in that their hearts would sink
But even a boy our Father knew
Would enjoy just a touch of blue.

Why God Created Pink

God made so many lovely colors
When He created the world
But I think He must have created pink
Just for little girls!

He knew how lovely their rosy lips
Would fit in each tiny face
And how soft their baby arms
Would feel in Mom's embrace.

He created their love and laughter,
And gave them sweet little voices
He made little girls so sweet
Oh, God made such wonderful choices!

And when He looked at all the colors
His decision was (I like to think)
For little girls so delicate and lovely
He would create the perfect color--PINK!

?

I Love Him Mommy

I love to watch my little brother
As he is sleeping in his bed
And every time I get the chance
I kiss his little head.

Your Child, God's Blessing

I watched you as you nursed your newborn son
And snuggled him close to you.
He was not the "perfect" child you planned
What had God given you?

Where was the child that you dreamed of?
And what would happen to your dreams for him?
How does God choose the child for parents
That He would send to them?

Perhaps God looked into your heart
And saw something good and true
And knew that his beloved treasure
Would be safe with you.

We teach our children daily
All the things they need to know
But sometimes it takes a special child
To help us really grow.

A special child can teach us so much
And God counts them jewels in His plan
And only when you've been blessed by one
Can you begin to understand.

I believe that in God's plan
He searched the whole earth through
To find the perfect parents for this child
And decided to bless you.

A special child can teach us so much
And God counts them jewels in His plan...

Your Eyes

My little one, your eyes are so green
Sparkling like emeralds in the light
Filled with love and promise
And in everything seeing delight.

Sweet baby, when I look into your eyes
My heart leaps from the love I feel
For I know that I look into your soul
And I can't believe this blessing can be real.

I pray that forever your eyes will be
Filled with the love and tenderness I see
And you will see that same immensity of love
Reflected back to you from the eyes of me.

I believe the eyes are mirrors of the soul
And their tenderness we don't control.
I believe that God in Heaven above
Has filled your heart and soul
and let your angelic eyes reflect His love.

Your Eyes

My little one, your eyes are so bright
Sparkling like diamonds in the light
Filled with love and promise
And in everything seeing delight.

Sweet baby, when I look into your eyes
My heart leaps from the love I feel
For I know that I look into your soul
And I can't believe this blessing can be real.

I pray that forever your eyes will be
Filled with the love and tenderness I see
And you will see that same immensity of love
Reflected back to you from the eyes of me.

I believe the eyes are mirrors of the soul
And their tenderness we don't control.
I believe that God in Heaven above
Has filled your heart and soul
and let your angelic eyes reflect His love.

Your Eyes

My little one, your eyes are so blue
Sparkling like sapphires in the light
Filled with love and promise
And in everything seeing delight.

Sweet baby, when I look into your eyes
My heart leaps from the love I feel
For I know that I look into your soul
And I can't believe this blessing can be real.

I pray that forever your eyes will be
Filled with the love and tenderness I see
And you will see that same immensity of love
Reflected back to you from the eyes of me.

I believe the eyes are mirrors of the soul
And their tenderness we don't control.
I believe that God in Heaven above
Has filled your heart and soul
And let your angelic eyes reflect His love.

You're Just a Baby Now

You are just a baby now
And I'm bigger than you are
You are too tiny to swing
Or share a candy bar.

But when you grow a little bigger
The two of us will play
And we will be the best of friends
Each and every day.

We will play hide and seek
And swing and slide together
And we will do puzzles indoors
When there is stormy weather.

I can hardly wait until
You're as big as me
We will always stick together
Just you wait and see!

I Will Always Lift You Up

I will always lift you up
No matter what you do
If your days grow cloudy
Or when your skies are blue.

My arms are here to hold you
And lift you toward the sky
I will teach you all I know
And give you your wings to fly!

Tiny Little Tushies

Tiny little tushies
Hanging out of little undies
No matter how hard I try
To keep them clean and neat and dry.

Undies put on by little hands
And sometimes wrong side out
Backwards is a frequent flaw
Fitting badly without a doubt.

Someday I will look back on the photos
That I don't share with just everyone
And smile when I see that precious tiny tushie
In the photos of my son.

Sweetest Kisses

The sweetest kisses on the earth
Come from babes to whom you gave birth.
Sweetest goo's and coo's are they
With which a baby starts her day!

The most cherished words whispered in my ear
Were the sweetest I could hear.
"Mommy, here's a kiss for you...
Do you have one for me too?"

How I love the thrill of you
The cuddly, awesome feel of you
And one of the most wonderful things I do
Is to share those baby kisses!

I Love You Head to Toe

I love your little baby face
With kissable cheeks and lips
Your precious little earlobes
And tiny finger tips!

I love your chubby little tum
Each dainty hand
With dimpled wrist
And each tiny little thumb.

I love your chubby little legs
With dimpled knees so cute
I love everything about
Your little birthday suit!

I love your little eyes so sweet
And each of your precious little feet.
I love your sweet little kissable nose—
I love you from your head to your toes!!

?

I love your chubby little legs
With dimpled knees so cute
I love everything about
Your little birthday suit!

Waiting for Baby

With my hand on that part of me that is a
home to you I stand here in awesome solitude
Alone? Not really...for you are with me.
Within me now but only weeks or days or hours
from now....you will be with me and we will no longer
be connected in one body as we are now but will
have a special connection all the same.
I feel the swell of my belly and a thrill runs through
me that sends goosebumps to my soul—I will be...
no I am...a mother. Just as much I as will be when
I hold you finally In my arms and stroke your head
Yes, I am already your mother...Your Mother
For all of these months I have held you in my body
And for even longer I have held you in my heart.
Rest now little one and enjoy your solitude
For a great big world awaits you...
As do your mommy's arms...

Nursing at My Breast

My motherly heart was softened
More than I could ever realize
With the first look I took
Into my newborn's eyes.

My nurturing love is in full bloom
And I am my motherly best
When I am cradling my child
Who is nursing at my breast.

75

Little Sweetheart

You are so sweet
And tiny and new
Everything is so
Perfect about you.

I look in awe
And tears start to fall
As I am overwhelmed
With the joy of it all.

So, I kiss you
Gently on your tiny head
And place you lovingly
Back in your little bed.

But my heart is filled
Up to the top
With a love for you
That will never stop.

?

J   is for Jacob the cutest little thing alive
A   is for Always Active and on busyness
    he seems to thrive
C   is for Carefree, Cheerful and full of
    childish exuberance and joy
O   is for Our darling Heaven sent little
    boy so full of fun and energy
B   is for Beautiful, and Boisterous Boy of
    ours who means the world to me!

Baby Booties

Tiny little booties
So precious and so sweet
How wonderfully soft are they
On my little one's feet...
Human hands made tiny little socks
For the little one I love
But the precious one who wears them
Was made by God above.
Oh God, I love Thy handiwork !
I'm in awe of all I see,
Especially such a dainty masterpiece
As the child in front of me!

Sweetest Things

Of the sweet things
I loved the best
I loved you snuggled
At my breast.
There was no sweeter
More precious time
Than cuddling you
Sweet child of mine.
Now you are bigger
And sip from your cup
No more need for Mommy
To snuggle you up.
But precious and sweet
Forever they will be
The memories of breastfeeding
With just you and me!

Little Kissy Face

I love the way you kiss me
I love your kissy face
The way you give mommy kisses
And snuggle in my embrace.

"Mommy Kisses" is all I say
And you start to come my way
With eyes all sweetly aglow
How much it thrills me
You just don't know!

Someday when you are a mommy too
And your little one gives to you
"Mommy kisses" on face and chin...
Then you will understand...

?

I love the way you kiss me
I love your kissy face
The way you give mommy kisses
And snuggle in my embrace.

Welcome to Your Room

Welcome little one
To your room
We made it just for you
It had to be just perfect
For nothing else would do!

For 9 months you snuggled
Close to this heart of mine
And now this little baby's nest
I created and designed.

Welcome precious little one
And soon you will come to know
All sorts of wonderful and delightful things
As you live and learn and grow.

Bless This Room

God bless this little room
And station Heavenly angels near
To protect the precious child
So sweetly nestled here.

God bless this little room
Each dainty little part
And keep my baby as safe here
As when she was snuggled near my heart...

God Bless this
Little Room

BIRTHDAY POEMS AND DITTIES

I love birthdays! As of Feb 2004, I have had 59 of them! When I was in grade school, I would begin asking for a birthday party around the middle of January. We lived on a farm until I was twelve and I didn't have very many birthday parties until we moved to the larger town of Paducah, Ky.

It wasn't the presents that necessarily appealed to me, but rather, the gathering together of all my friends and family in one place at one time. I have always loved that part of birthdays!

I get requests almost every day requesting poems for and about birthdays. I respond with party invitations, song, poems and page ideas. I have written verses for the very young to the centenarian and to the families each birthday is just as special as the other.

I was running out of room and thought of omitting this chapter when my friend, Sharon, called and asked me if I had included it in my count. She insisted that you would want this chapter and would use it, so thanks to Sharon Hammond, it is included in the book in almost its entirety.

Milestones

Baby Album Poems

Look at me and you will see
That I'm having lots of fun
And life can only get better
'Cause I've just begun!

In this album are the photos
Of me from the very start
Including ones taken at my beginning
When I nestled near Mommy's heart!

On My Way to ONE!

My first six months
I'm pleased to say
Helped me get started
Now I'm on my way...

I'm on my way
To being one
And completing
A whole year of fun!

?

I'm on my way...
A year has past
And today I find
I'm ONE at last!

As Your First Year Ends

When God sends an angel down to earth
We call this heavenly miracle... birth.

You grow sweeter with each passing day
How much you're loved... no words can say.

We hold your hand and you hold our heart
From the innermost tender part.

We watch you with love beyond what we've known
Amazed at what our love has sown.

This first year ends and we celebrate anew
The joy God brought us when He sent us YOU!

?

You are Mommy's angel
So precious and dear
I can hardly believe
That we've loved you a year!

We celebrate the year
That we've had you to love
Our angel, our princess
Our gift from above!

One Year Old

We loved you before you were born.
We waited for 9 long months
To see your face
And give you a long awaited
First loving embrace.

Now that we loved and cuddled you
For a whole year today
We can hardly believe the miracle
That God sent our way.
You are our one year old blessing
Is all I can say
As we celebrate your first birthday!

?

It's my birthday
And I'm so excited!
I got lots of presents
And I was delighted!

Missed Birthdays of One and Two

This page is in honor of you
When you were one and when you were two!
I have no photos to place in this part
But the memories are stored forever
Safely in my heart!

I wish you could take a look
But, alas, a heart is not the same as a book
But each mother has such treasures there
To ponder, cherish, treasure and share.

All gentle memories whether large or small
Are recorded forever, once and for all!
I will try as diligently as I can do
To share these special memories with you.

For you are my source of happiness and joy
And have been since you were a tiny baby boy.
The fact that we have no photos of that day
Does not diminish the value of that time in any way!

I replay those times over and over in my head
Along with sweet memories of putting you to bed,
Of feeding you your bottle, of kissing your baby cheek
And of listening to the first words I ever heard you speak.

Your accomplishments are special to me
As is everything you do
And this is to make note of those special days
In this special book of YOU!

This page is in honor of you when You were one and when you were two!

Walking Into Two

I hold back sentimental tears
At the most precious view
As my little one year old
Walks out of One and into Two.

One was an adventure
With days that were all too few
Precious little infant days
Gone now that you are Two.

I hold back my tears and smile again
For my heart always smiles at you
And I will adjust to the fact
As all moms do—-
That my darling is now Two!

?

Two

Happy Birthday little one
We are so glad today
To bring out the cake and candles
To celebrate your birthday!

We wondered what could be more fun
Than watching you as you turned one...
But an even more exciting thing to do
Is to celebrate your turning TWO!

Turning Two

Some say that turning one is nice
And it cannot be beat
For the first birthday that you celebrate
Is a joy that is unique!

But I think that you have the best
And most wonderful day today
For even though one was fun
TWO is the best birthday!

You know that there will be goodies
Cake and ice cream too
And all of the gifts that people bring
Will each one be for you!

So happy birthday little one
Enjoy your day today
And may joy and happiness
Bless your life every day!

Turning Three

Some say that turning two is nice
And it cannot be beat
And celebrating your birthday
Is a joy that is unique!

But I think that you have the best
And most wonderful day today
For even though two was fun
THREE is the best birthday!

A Big Boy Birthday

Yesterday or day before
(or maybe a few days more)
I was only one year old
And was rather small
(So I've been told!)
Today I am a boy of two
And there are
So many things
That I can do
But tomorrow when
From my nap I awake
I'll help my mommy
Bake a birthday cake.
For tomorrow will be
A super duper day
Fun in such a special way
'Cause it will be my third birthday!!
Hey! Look at ME!
Today I'm THREE!
I'm as happy
As a kid can be!

Happy Birthday Little One

We are so glad today
To bring out the cake and candles
To celebrate your birthday!
We wondered what could be
A more exciting thing to do
Than watching you as you turned two
But now your joy is plain to see
The best birthday is turning THREE!

Today is the Day

Today is the day before my birthday
And I'm as excited as can be
I will go to sleep as a two year old
And when I awake I will be Three!

Three means lots of big boy stuff
And lots of brand new things
I can hardly wait for the end of two
So I can see what three will bring!

Four

Happy Birthday
And Many more
For a darling little girl
Who is turning FOUR!

?

Yesterday and day before
I was only three
But soon I will celebrate
A happy day for me!

For tomorrow when
From my rest I awake
I'll help my mommy
Bake a birthday cake.

For tomorrow will be
A super duper day
Fun in such a special way
Cause it will be my fourth birthday!!

Mom's Reflection

I am not a sentimental person
Don't cry at movies so sad
Don't worry about the good guys
If they will defeat the bad.
But though I used to be unemotional
And considered myself tough enough
Now when I see more candles on your cake
My heart just turns to mush!
Each candle represents another year
And less time for you to remain
The tiny dependent little person
That you were when you came!

Happy Birthday Teen

Look at you!
You are all grown up!
A teenager at last!
And I sit in amazement
That the time has gone so fast!

From the day I first held you
And wiped baby tears away
How could the years go so quickly
That brought us to this day!

I do not want to hold you back
I know that you must grow
I will love you at 2 or 20
Just wanted you to know!

My Sixteen Year Old Daughter

Look at you preening in the mirror
Glancing into an open screen
That seems not quite adult or child
But somewhere in between.

You've changed so much
In this last year or so
I've watched you blossom
And watched you grow.

And it makes me teary
As today I finally realize
You are only a child
In your mommy's eyes.

So, my sixteen year old baby
I congratulate you today
And amid all of your other admiring fans
Send my birthday wishes your way.

I wish for you love, joy and peace
And happiness without end
And that you will always have in your life
A trusted and loyal friend.

You've changed so much
In this last year or so
I've watched you blossom
And watched you grow.

Sixteen is the Perfect Age

For fifteen years
I've been a kid
And I traveled by foot or bike
But once I hit the big sixteen
I can drive anytime I like!

For fifteen years
They called me kid
With little respect for me
But once I hit the big sixteen
I'm grown up...
Anyone can plainly see!

50 Fabulous Years!

Life begins at 50...
At least that's what they say
And I really do believe it
For I had a terrific day!

You won't hear me complain
That I am getting old and gray
I'm here to celebrate
Another wonderful day!

You won't see me pout
Because I've hit the big 5- 0
But you will see me smiling
Everywhere I go!

For my life is just beginning
And I'm having so much fun
That I can hardly wait
To celebrate fifty-one!

58th Birthday Poem

For many years I wondered
Just how wise I'd be
When at last Maturity
Would catch up with me.

I thought in my twenties
That I was very wise
But as I hit my thirties
I knew it was only in my eyes...

Forties came and I can tell you
It was with a sudden blow
That I realized the more I knew
The more I knew I did not know!

And with my fifties came a rush
Of new interest and yearnings
To do something more creative and insightful
And to pursue something I found delightful!

And when my prayer was answered
And retirement came my way
It added cause for celebration
To my 58th birthday!

So now I am without a job
To go to every day
But I will welcome and embrace
What the Good Lord sends my way!

For many years I wondered
Just how wise I'd be...

Happy 80th Birthday to My Grandma

When God gave you to this family
He gave us so very much
He gave us love in human form
To kiss and hug and touch.

For 80 years you've been here
And you touched the hearts of those you've met.
This little book is to show you
That those who love you don't forget.

Our prayer is that it blesses you
To look upon each page inside.
And know that when we say "Our Grandma"
We say it with love and pride!

We love you!

Welcome to the Club
(As You Mature)

Little jars of moisturizer
Sitting in a row
Lipsticks on the counter
Colors all aglow...
Powder and blushes, at the ready
Masks should be close at hand
Wrinkle removers at attention
Ready on demand...
Base, concealer, tweezers, pencils
Ah...and a "Tricks the Stars Use" book
All necessary to achieve...
That daily "Natural Look!"

I Don't Fret About Birthdays

Don't celebrate birthdays...
Don't need to anymore!
Don't need the calendar to remind me
Of the good things God has in store!

Don't need to worry about my birthday
Or fret about the date
God will do all things in His time
And He is never late!

Family Birthdays

Happy Birthday to Mom

Mom, I love you so very much.
You give my life a gentle touch
That can only come through
A wonderful blessing such as you!

So I celebrate your birth today
And hope your wishes come true.
I thank God daily for giving me
A wonderful Mom like you!

I thank God daily for giving me
A wonderful Mom like you!

Birthday Blessings for A Special Mother in Law

You have always been a blessing
You have always been a dear
And you are a source of joy
That gets more special every year!

God gave the world such a lovely gift
When He sent an angel such as you
Your loved ones thank Him on your birthday
And the whole year through!

You have treated everyone with kindness
And showered them with love
With gentleness and tenderness
That comes only from above.

May your loved ones surround you
On your very special day
And may the Father up in Heaven
Answer every prayer you pray!

And may this birthday be a blessing
That will fill your heart up to the top
With joy, love and happiness
That will never stop!!

God gave the world such a lovely gift
When He sent an angel such as you...

Mother in Law

I pity the person
Indeed I do
Who doesn't have
A mother in law
Like YOU!

One of the greatest gifts
I have ever received
Is something only you could give
And it will be my most treasured gift
For as long as I shall live.

On this day as we celebrate
The wonderful occasion of your birth
I just want to let you know
You're the best Mother in law on earth!

?

I pity the person
Indeed I do
Who doesn't have
A mother in law
Like YOU!

Happy Birthday Sister

I searched and searched for something
To give you on your special day
But nothing was quite good enough
Or not the words I wanted to say!
I looked in the stores to find
That perfect little gift
Something very special
To give your heart a lift.

I looked in the bookstores,
And even Wal-Mart too...
Nothing there could come close
To being special enough for you.
I looked in the ads of the newspapers
I even looked online
Praying that somewhere
A special gift for you I'd find.

Then I felt a gentle nudge
That gave me quite a start
T'was if a voice said to me
"Look within your heart!"
So I looked inside my heart
At all the memories there
Of all the wonderful loving
Memories that we share.

And I came up with this little verse
That is so simple yet so true
The best thing about being sisters
Is that for a sister I have YOU!

Teacher Birthday

Happy Birthday Special Ed Teacher

Words just don't seem to be
Adequate to say
How wonderful you are
In every single way!

Words fail me when I try
To say that I am proud...
I hear them in my heart
But they seem inadequate out loud.

I've watched you through the years
When times were really tough
And when others might have quit
And said enough is enough.

But you carried on and followed through
And you make such a difference every day
In all the young and special lives
That our Father sends your way.

I pray that on your birthday
And each day your whole life through
That blessing upon blessing
God will bestow on you!!

You make such a difference every day...

Birthday Blessings

Birthday Prayer for You

Sometimes our lives bring things
That we don't understand
And it is difficult to see
Just where was the Master's Hand.

But God will work all things out
If we just give him the chance to do
The things He knows are the best
And then He will see us through.

So my birthday prayer for you
Is that God above would bless
Your life, your day your very being
With peace, joy, love and happiness!

?

May today be the day
You dreamed of yesterday
And may it be much more.

May the joy of this happy day
Be only the beginning
Of the joy you have in store!

Birthday Blessings

You have always been a blessing
You have always been a dear
And you are a source of joy
That gets more special every year!

God gave the world such a lovely gift
When He sent an angel such as you
Your loved ones thank him on your birthday
And the whole year through!

You have treated everyone with kindness
And showered them with love
With gentleness and tenderness
That comes only from above.

May your loved ones surround you
On your very special day
And may the Father up in Heaven
Answer every prayer you pray!

And may this birthday be a blessing
That will fill your heart up to the top
With joy, love and happiness
That will never stop!!

May your day be blessed with sunshine
And filled with joy and love
And may God shower you with blessings
And bless all of those you love!

You have always been a blessing
You have always been a dear...

May roses kissed with sunshine
Glistening in the morning's dew
Be only half as wonderful
As the day in store for you!

May your birthday be the best one yet
But may every year be even better
Than the one of the year before
And may you relish every blessing
That the Lord has in store!

May your days be full of sunshine
And peace and joy and love
And God bless you daily
And bless all of those you love!!

?

You are special and loved so much
You give my life a gentle touch
That can only come through
A wonderful blessing such as you!

So I celebrate your birth today
And hope your wishes come true
For mine already have
In getting to know wonderful you!

?

May your day be blessed with sunshine
And filled with joy and love
And may God shower you with blessings
And bless all of those you love!

May God look down from Heaven above
And bless your day with peace and love.
My dear friend, I love you so,
And I'm taking a moment to let you know!

May God bless you in every way
And may love and joy fill this day!
You are a joy and a treasure too.
Each day I thank the Lord for you!

?

If I could sing a song for you
I'd sing it loud and clear
I'd wish you a happy birthday
In tones so sweet and clear!

But since I'm not a singer
And can't sing that song for you
I will just send a little blessing
And hope this verse will do!

May God grant you peace and joy
And send blessings to you each day
To fill your life with happiness
With flowers strewn along with way!

?

Have a blessed birthday
And may your joy overflow
You are a treasured friend
And I just wanted you to know!

May God look down
From Heaven above
And bless your day
With peace and love

?

May this birthday be the turning
Of bad things into good
May all your thoughts and wishes
Suddenly be understood.

May things that have perplexed you
Have solutions and be controlled
And may you in every endeavor
Finally reach your goals.

And may life daily be a blessing
Each and every part
And there be joy in your household
And in your precious heart!!

?

This may not be the first wish
And surely won't be the last
To wish that your every
Dream comes true
Before this year has past!

Just wishing you
The most special day today
With multitudes of blessings
To come your way.

May you prosper
And may you have peace
And love and harmony
That will never cease.

?

Hope your year is wonderful
Hope your day is bright
And that the blessings you received today
Last far into the night!

And tomorrow when you awake
May a smile form on your lips
And may not a bit of birthday cake
Settle on your hips!!!

?

May today be the day you dreamed of yesterday
And may it be much more.
May the joy of this happy day
Be only the beginning of the joy you have in store!

Just wishing you the
Most special day today...

You are special and loved so much
You give my life a gentle touch
That can only come through
A wonderful blessing such as you!

So I celebrate your birth today
And hope your wishes come true
For mine wishes already have
In getting to know wonderful you!

?

May God richly bless you
And all of those held dear
With joy and peace and happiness
Today and throughout the year!!

?

May this birthday be a happy one
The best that you've had yet
Filled with wonderful surprises
That you will never forget!

So I celebrate your birth today
And hope your wishes come true
For mine wishes already have
In getting to know wonderful you!

From All of Us

Happy Birthday to our friend
And best wishes for the day
To bring just the sort of fun
That you're hoping for your way!

We treasure your friendship
Indeed we do!
And we treasure the gift
That is uniquely you!

May your day be special
And your dreams come true
This our birthday wish
Especially for you!

?

Happy Birthday special friend
And may your whole life through
You remember how much you are loved
By those who send loving wishes to you!

?

Hope you know that we are here
To bring to your day some added cheer!
We love you bunches and want to say
We hope you have a joy filled day!
We ask the Lord above to bless
Your day with joy and happiness!!

Happy Birthday Ladies
On this your special day
Hope everything is wonderful
With sunny skies your way!

We want you to feel special
And to know that we care
About your special day today
And your joy we want to share!

?

We are your friends
Who love you so
And we're taking this moment
To let you know!

Have a blessed birthday
And may your joy overflow
We treasure your friendship
And just wanted you to know!

?

You are special
In every way
We hope you enjoy
This wonderful day!

May you be blessed
In all you do
On this your birthday
And all year through!

Happy Birthday to our friend
And best wishes for the day
To bring just the sort of fun
That you're hoping for your way!

We treasure your friendship
And all the things you do
And we treasure most, the gift
That is uniquely you!

May your day be special
And your dreams come true
This our birthday wish
Especially for you!

?

It's a very special day
That's why all of us would say
May your day be richly blessed
With love and peace and happiness!

And may the joy that you have found
Cause joy in others to abound
And may the day bring a special treat
Something excitingly unique!

?

Have a blessed birthday
And may your joy overflow
We treasure your friendship
And just wanted you to know!

We are all here to say
You deserve a wonderful day!
And may your birthday be
The best day yet in history!

May God look down
From His Heaven above
And less you
And all those you love!

?

It's your special day today
And we celebrate with you.
We hope your day will be the best
With blessings through and through!

And with the coming of the night
As you snuggle in your bed
May happy thoughts of your fun day
Be replayed in your head!

?

Hip Hip Hooray!
It's your special day!
We are celebrating with you
Because that's what good friends do!!

May your day be the very best
And may your whole life be blessed!!

Happy Birthday dear friend
We are here to say
We wish for you the very best
On your special day!

May God richly bless you
And all of those you love
And may you feel His love
Shining on you from above!

?

Happy Birthday dear friend
We are here to say
We wish for you the very best
On your special day!

We pray God's mercy and His grace
To last your whole life through
And ask that today would be
A blessed one for you!

?

Today we celebrate with you
This very special day
And ask that God would send
Special blessings on their way!

We pray that He would bless
Your home and family too
And make everyday as special
As the special treasure that is you!

May God bless you
In every way
And may love and joy
Fill this day!

You are a joy
And a treasure too
And daily we thank
Our God for you!

Online Friends

Happy Birthday My Computer Guy

If your name were "Mac"
I'd give you an "apple" for your special day
And once you had unwrapped it
I'd take a "byte" away.

But you are my special guy
And mean so much to me
That I'm celebrating your birthday
By upgrading your PC!

So get with the program
And have a happy day
We will celebrate in style
And Drive all your cares away!

Happy Birthday !

What a wonderful day for a birthday!
And how wonderful that we get to share
On your special day
In a special cyber way
And with a little birthday prayer
That God would bless this day
And every day for you
With blessings for your birthday
And each day the whole year through!

?

If I could sing a song for you
I'd sing it loud and clear
I'd sing about your special day
And the fact that you're held dear!

But instead I'll have to write a note
And join your friends online
In wishing a happy birthday
To a special friend of mine!

?

We feel so very blessed
Yes, indeed we do
To count among our friends online
A special friend like you.
We pray for birthday blessings
To surround you all day long
That will put a smile upon your face
And in your heart a song!

Belated Birthday

Even though your birthday is over
And the night has come
May the first day at your new age
Be happy from the first rising of the sun!

May God send blessing upon blessing
Today and the whole year through
And may His blessings show
Just how special he holds you!

?

Sorry that my wish is late
But please don't worry
Love and prayers and wishes
Are not to be in a hurry!

My wish for you on this special day
And each day the whole year though
Would be that all your fondest dreams
Would finally come true!

May God look upon you
With His love and Grace
And may His loving arms surround
With a warm embrace.

Sorry that my wish is late
But please don't worry...

CHRISTMAS

Christmas is my most favorite time of the year. I love the reason for the season, the way that the whole world is aware of the season and the way it seems to bring out the good in everyone.

One of the first verses that I ever remember writing was written when I was in fourth grade and was about Christmas. My mom sent it to the local paper and it was published.

I remember that Mom was sad because they published the Poet Laureate of Ky's poem the week of Christmas and not mine. She wanted mine to be in the paper to surprise me. I always teased her about her thinking I should be the Poet Lureate! (Aren't Moms wonderful!)

A Christmas Prayer

Lord, please create a cradle in my heart
Where Baby Jesus can be born
And let the love within me
Be enough to keep Him warm...

And Father let Your love flow through me
In such a special way
That the wonderful joy of Christmas
Would stay with me every day!

Oh, make my heart a worthy place
For the child to come and stay
And I thank you for that Greatest Gift
You gave us on Christmas Day!

Manger to the Cross

Tiny little Baby Jesus in a manger born
In a little tray where the cattle ate their corn.
Tiny little baby came to save us every one
Who would welcome the little one...
Who would welcome God's only son?

Tiny little baby grew up to be a man
Evil nails maimed Him and pierced His hand.
Who would console Him, who would be the one
Who would comfort Him, God's only son?

Celebrate the baby but celebrate the man
Celebrate the sacrifice of the nailed scared hand.
Celebrate the birth of the one who came to give
His life on an awful tree that the rest of us might live.

On this most special day of the year
We want to share with those we hold dear
The joy, the peace and happiness
That comes from God above.
May you and your family be blessed by
The joy of knowing God's love.

On This Most Special Day
of the Year
We Want to Share with
Those We Hold Dear...

The Glow

Oh, what if I had missed this glow
And of such beauty would never know
Thankfully I did not miss the sight
Of your sweet face by candle light.

Your face in innocence glows and shines
As the light your face defines
Each beam kisses your sweet face
and lingers there in sweet embrace.

The candle flame has done its part
Reflecting in its tiny spark
The sweetness of your tender heart.
Never will I forget the sight
Of my sweet child by candlelight...

Tree Trimming Party

We want to share our joy with those we hold dear
In this wonderful and special time of year!
Good friends with happy memories
We invite you to help us trim our tree.

Please come and help and share our glee
And bring an ornament for the tree.
It will be treasured for years to come
And will make this day a very special one!

Never will I forget the sight
Of my sweet child by candlelight...

Christmas Eve

Going to Grandparents' for Christmas Eve
Is something we love to do
We enjoy the visit on Christmas Eve
And look forward to it all year through!

Grandma and Grandpa
Love us so much
They kiss our cheeks and
Our faces they touch.

We love to open up gifts
And their beautiful tree
Is always a delightful
And wonderful sight to see.

But this the
Most wonderful part,
They listen to us
From the depth of their hearts!

?

We love to open up gifts
And their beautiful tree
Is always a delightful
And wonderful sight to see.

Country Christmas

A little secret I must confess
A Country Christmas is the best
Filled with wonderful holiday fun
That makes the day for everyone.
We plan the day for months before
It is the day we wait all year for
And when it comes we all agree
That it is the best day there could be!

Kinfolks come from miles around
Leaving the city and getting out of towns
And they knock at our door with smiling faces
And get lost in the huddles and cuddles and embraces.
We've cleaned and cooked and wrapped all night
So that we can be up before it's light
And snuggle in pj's and robes and such
As the gifts we open and share and touch.

The breakfast will be hot and served with laughter
And then we will start preparations right after
For the biggest dinner that you could think up
With treats for everyone right down to the pup!
Oh, I pity the city folks who live in town
Whose Christmas starts off with a traffic frown
And who must buy a turkey all frozen and stiff
And shop at the mall for a Christmas gift.

I pity the folks with the artificial tree
When the whole green woods is there for me!
I love the gift making and the homemade fun
That make the day special for everyone.
Yes, I love my Christmas I must admit
For me a Country Christmas is the very best fit!!

A Kitty's Christmas

Christmas Is Purr-fection
It just cannot be beat.
My stocking is filled to the brim
With the very "micest" treats!

My humans really love me.
They are the cat's meow.
They treat me so specially
Like I'm their favorite pal!

I feel badly for the other cats
Who don't not live with me
For my Christmas was just purr-fect.
I'm as contented as can be!!

Catty Remarks

I love Christmas
I love the excitement and fun
I love my new toys
And sleeping in the sun.

?

My humans really love me.
They are the cat's meow.
They treat me so specially
Like I'm their favorite pal!

119

Christmas Wrapture

Oh look, the tree is up
That means that Christmas is coming
Daddy is smiling ear to ear...
And Mommy is humming!

Oh look, the lights are on the tree
And the presents we are wrapping...
I think more presents appear
While we kids are napping!

Oh look, the kitchen is getting busy
Mommy is cleaning and cooking...
We see her sampling the food
When she thinks we aren't looking!

Oh look, the calendar says it's Christmas Eve
And we are so excited
We look forward to the morning
I know we will be delighted!

LOOK!

Look at all the packages
Underneath the tree
I know that lots of them
Are especially for me!

Oh look, the tree is up
That means that Christmas
Is coming...

Joys of Christmas

Years come and go
So very fast
But Christmas memories
Always last.

Mistletoe and shiny bells
Hung on tree or post
Hugs and kisses and teddy bears
Are some memories treasured most.

Christmas comes but once a year
For babies, grandparents, man or wife
But the memories created in that time
Last you all of your life.

Our Family

Our family through the years
Has had it's share of laughter and of tears
But whatever we do and whatever the weather
We will come through the storms ot lite together.

?

Years come and go
So very fast
But Christmas memories
Always last.

Christmas Pj's

Every year at Christmas
We do a special thing
We wear Christmas Pj's
That Santa always brings!

It started when we were little
And our tradition has become
We love our Christmas jammies
Just like when we were young!

The little ones get sleepers
And the teens get stylish threads
While Mom gets a nightie
And Gramma gets flannel...red!

Dad and Grampy's favorites are traditional
With piping on the yoke
And sometimes Mom gets him Santa silky ones
But we know it is a joke!

We may have trends that come and go
As our family changes and grows
But come Christmas it's pajama time
And everybody knows!

It started when we were little
And our tradition has become
We love our Christmas jammies
Just like when we were young!

Choosing a Tree

I awoke this morning
Happy as could be
'Cause today is the day
When we choose our tree!

We will all go together
And look until we drop
For a tree that will hold
Our angel at its top!

The tree must be special
And it must be tall and strong
To stand inside our living room
Guarding presents all month long!

So off we go to choose our tree
Can you tell that I'm excited?
Can't wait until it's in our home
Decorated, trimmed and lighted!!

Christmas Blessing

May your Christmas be blessed
With joy and peace and happiness.
And may God's precious gift to you
Bless you today and the whole year through.

The tree must be special
And it must be tall and strong...

Santa's Wonderland

Way up North is a place they say
That Santa and his reindeer stay.
It is a very happy land
That is fun, unique and very grand.

They say that Santa has a shop
Where all year long work never stops
And toys of all kinds line it's shelves
All hand made by little elves.

They say the snow falls all year long
And happy folks sing Christmas songs
And whistle merrily as they go
At least they tell me this is so.

They say that reindeer fly and paw
The most beautiful that you ever saw.
With one whose nose is brightest red
To guide the way for Santa's sled.

They say the place is always the same
And say that Santa knows your name
And that this is his home each day
As he waits for Christmas to come your way.

They say that's where Santa's Sleigh
Is polished and oiled
And shined up so bright
To get it ready for Christmas Eve Night.

Well, I can't say for sure that this is so
But it was told to me by someone
Who should know....

Little Christmas Ditties

Mommy's job is to cook and bake
And make cookies for us all.
Her job includes a lot of trips
For shopping at the mall.

Mommy also bakes the turkey
To make sure it turns out right
And Daddy's job is best of all
He puts up all the lights!

?

I'm so sad and nothing can cheer me
I would cry but Santa might hear me
We moved into an awful place
Sure it looks great but
THERE'S NO FIREPLACE!

?

I saw a kid crying at the mall
And ask what was the matter
He said his daddy wouldn't buy
A great big tall stepladder.

So how would Santa get to his roof
If his sleigh stopped on the ground
For from all the pictures that he saw
Santa Clause was big and round!

A Christmas Prayer for You

Sometimes our lives bring things
That we don't understand
And it is difficult to see
Just where was the Master's Hand.

But God will work all things out
If we just give him the chance to do
The things He knows are the best
And then He will see us through.

So my Christmas prayer for you
Is that God above would bless
Your life, your day, your very being
With peace, joy, love and happiness!

Your First Christmas Together

If Christmas has always been wonderful
A time cherished and special to see
Sharing your first Christmas together
Will show you how lovely it can be.

Each bough of the tree becomes important
Each light and each ornament so fine
Reminds you of your love for each other
And love and tenderness in your faces shine.

This is your first "married" Christmas
And so lovely is the sweet memory
That I know you look forward to the coming years
So you can see just how marvelous it will be!

126

First Christmas

Look at the sparkles in your eyes!
How wonderful to see
As in awe and wonder
You see the lighted Christmas tree!

Look at the smile on your sweet face
Oh, I love that look!
Your tiny little face looks like
A picture in a book!

Your little arms reaching out to us
For hugs and cuddles and such
This is the kind of Christmas joy
That we can hold and touch!

Quite lovely for one to see
Are the lighted ornaments on our tree
But better yet and more precious still
Is the precious face I see!

I've recorded this moment in my mind
And in my heart today
This is a moment I'll treasure forever,
The memory of your first Christmas Day!

?

Look at the sparkles in your eyes
How wonderful to see!

FUN STUFF

Everyone needs a bit of fun and downright silliness in their lives. Before I entered this bliss of retirement, I remember how the mood of the office could be changed for the better with a light hearted comment or a joke.

I came from a family that teased each other and had a lot of fun. Some of my earliest memories of other than my family are of the neighbors teasing me. Being a little farm girl, the old standby joke was to ask me if my daddy still stole chickens. Of course I would say, "NO," immediately in defense of my dad and they would then say, "Oh, when did he stop?" Then I decided one day to say, "Yes!" That must be the right answer, I reasoned since the other one was wrong. Then they all laughed because I just said my dad was stealing chickens.

I was perplexed or as a child I guess I was just plain confused!! What was the right answer—how could I tell them my daddy was not stealing chickens?? My mom said "Honey, they are just teasing you. You can't win at that game. Listen to the question." AH HA! The lights went on and I realized that I had to beat them at their own game.

In the midst of a crowded country store, the question was asked by someone with a twinkle in his eye— "So, Thena, does your daddy still steal chickens?" "My daddy has never stolen a chicken," I said, "and never will." The crowd roared and was proud of me that I had figured them out and played their game. Dad was pleased as punch and true to my word—he never stole a chicken!!

If You See My Wife in Wal-Mart

If you see my wife in Wal-Mart
Please send her home to me.
The kids think she's been gone too long
And I'm starting to agree.

I don't know what's she's buying
Goodness knows she has it all.
She bought her Christmas paper
Two years ago last fall!

She has templates, she has paper
She has eyelets, she has string .
She has everything for scrapping
That could be sold to a human being!

She bought pumpkins in July
For October pages she will do
When she finishes her February pages
Of the children at the zoo!

It you see my wife in Wal-Mart
She will be in a hurry I guess
And you may not be able to stop her
If she's on the way to the LSS!

If you see my wife in Wal-Mart
Please send her home to me.
The kids think she's been gone too long
And I'm starting to agree.

Mom on Strike

There was a solemn air in the neighborhood
That had not been seen before
Husbands gathered together
In groups of three and four.

It was a horrible day for them
They raised their eyebrows in shock
And gave their condolences to
The saddest man on the block!

His wife had declared that week
Suddenly and out of the blue
That she was no longer working
And what things she would not do!

Things would have to change said she
The hired help was starting to roar
The carpet tread under foot
This mom would be no more!

The dishes sat in the dishwasher
With the dirty ones in the sink
And as far as laundry...
Well, the hamper was starting to stink...

The rugs were furry with dust bunnies
And the flowers in the pots began to die
And our mom sat there thinking
That he would notice by and by...

The beds were not made
And errands were not run
And if mamma's not happy
No one is... not one!

By day number two
And day number three
Dad found out
How miserable it could be.

So Mom is on strike
And is carrying her sign
She is a demonstrator
Walking the line.

Not one mom will cross it
Not one wife will say
That a mommy's day should be
All work and no play!

So jump in now hubbies
And help out your spouse
Or the Picket line could be forming
Right outside your house.....

?

Oh Sweetheart, love of my life
My wonderful and adorable wife,
Please drop your picket sign
And come home to me.
The children all miss you
And I ready to plea!

When A Cow Laughs

I was walking in the woods
On a lovely summer day
When ere I chanced to see
Two heifer cows at play.

They ran along the clover
And nibbled here and there
Then one nuzzled the other's ear
As if a joke to share.

It must have been a silly joke
That jarred her to her toes
For as I watch (and I lie not) she laughed so hard...
That MILK ran out her nose!!!

Chances are Remote...

You are all set for a nice evening at home
Your husband is there so you are not alone.
You cuddle up on the sofa to watch the tv
And what do you think the chances will be
Of your watching a show from beginning to end
Without the channel being changed again and again...
If your husband is there, then as I wrote
I'd say your changes are
REMOTE!

I was walking in the woods
On a lovely summer day...

Thena B.S. (Before Scrapping)

Time was when my house was clean
And my guest room was a lovely sight
With pillows tossed gently on the bed
To bring my guests delight.

Silk flowers adored the wall
And the comforter was down
My room was lavender, trimmed in white
And with great pleasure I glanced around.

It was such a lovely little room
That sometimes I would sneak in and read a book
Or perhaps 'tis where you would find me napping
That is, of course... until I took up scrapping!

Soon the lovely dainty desk
Would no longer do
We had to build my new one in the room
Because the door was too small to get it through!

The dresser soon was emptied of all clothes
(I gave them to Goodwill)
Because my software needed a home
And soon each drawer began to fill.

There was no room for the old fashion lamps
That looked so lovely there
Soon the dresser top held three (count'em) printers
With nary a smidge of room to spare!

The closet once full of dresses and blazers and such
Was blocked by Office Depot supplies
Such as little cubby hole shelves
Each cubby holding a scrapping surprise!

Cont....

133

I think my carpet is still lavender
But I rarely see it anymore
For I have stacks of scrapping mags
That are always stacked along the floor.

I have a little TV in the room
So the reality shows I can view
While I'm in my little scrapping room
And my TV show is due.

My dinning room is still quite full
Of my scrapping overflow
For our house is rather small
And there's nowhere else to grow...

I hope the neighbors don't complain
When our house begins to lean
From all the heavy scrapping supplies—
At least those supplies are clean...

I used to love to read novels
And non-fiction too
But it has been a while
Since I've read one all way through.

I tend to order Adobe manuals
And books on photography
And scrapping mags, card making mags
These now appeal more to me.

Some day perhaps my house will shine
And my addiction to scrapping will fade
And I feel the need to scrap no more
But enjoy the books I've made.

Cont...

Perhaps I shall pass the scrapping torch
Down to the next in line
And the scrapping inclination
My daughter will then find.

Ah, t'would be so nice to sit and rest
In a house so shinny and bright
And not have to fret should the doorbell ring
As I run to declutter both left and right.

But I shall enjoy my little world
Until that time should come again
And share my messy scrapping room woes
With my online scrapper friends.

And if you should ring my doorbell
Please allow me a bit of time
To clean a place for you to sit on the sofa
And remove all the portable scrapping stuff of mine....

?

It was such a lovely little room
That sometimes I would sneak
In and read a book
Or perhaps 'tis where you would
Find me napping
That is, of course...
Until I took up scrapping!

The Question:

Do you have stacks of goodies
Which you buy and hoard
Do you think of QVC
As your monthly scrap reward?

Don't worry dear scrapping friends
In this you are not alone
I am amazed at how much paper, cardstock,
And assorted "stuff" I own...

I have so many stickers
And assorted die cuts by the score.
I have quite enough scrap supplies
To start my own first class scrapping store...

I have Embellishments of metal
And ribbons of grosgrain
For when it comes to QVC
My impulses I cannot restrain...

Idea Books of every flavor
Fall off of my shelves
They must have been purchased
By some mischievous elves...

There are Gel pens, markers,
And stickers...oh my
I guess I will purchase them
Till their stack reaches the sky...

Perhaps I shall be immortalized someday
By a famous singer or rapper
It's especially disturbing since...
I'm a computer scrapper!

Anyone Else Have This Happen?

I awoke to the saddest sight...
All of my clothing shrunk last night!
I hung them in the closet
And then turned out the light
Only to find when I awoke
They had become smaller during the night!

It was the saddest thing to see
All of the things that had fit me
Were now much too tight and clung...
Do you think it was the way they were hung
That caused the shrinking in the night
Or could it have been the lack of light?

This has happened once before
(er..twice...ok three or four)
And I bought new stuff at the store.
And what an ugly surprise...
When I had to buy a larger size!

My slacks and blouses no longer fit
And to make the matter worse
Even my shoes were not immune
The only thing that fit me was my purse!

So I think I will be more careful in the future
Just where I hang my clothes at night
Because if all of this shrinking continues
I will look a sight!!

I hope the scientist will find an answer
As to what causes this awful problem soon
Because I've stored the clothes as evidence
And my closet is running out of room!

Company Down the Walk...

How special to be at home
On a lovely rainy day.
How perfect to put my feet up
But put nothing else away.

How nice to relax and say
I'll do the cleaning later on
How neat is the treat of playing
My very favorite song.

Oh, no, I looked out the window
Is that a familiar car?
Perhaps they aren't stopping here...
Ooops! They are!

Quick, someone grab the newspaper
And someone take the snacks
Someone close the closet door
And hang that coat up on a rack!

Oh, no ! There are dishes in the sink
And laundry is on the table
Someone throw it somewhere
As quick as you are able!

Someone run check the bathroom
And make sure the towels are clean
And the hamper isn't overflowing
And no cobwebs can be seen!

Someone unplug the sweeper
And someone let out the cat
And make sure the air is fresh
And put away that ball and bat!

Someone get the door
And smooth your hair a bit
And on your way don't trip
On my emergency sewing kit!

I'm looking out the window
And I see the car pull in
They look briefly at a map...
And then take off again!

So now I'm all conflicted
My day is thrown off track
And I must resume my cleaning
In case that car comes back!!

?

Oh, no, I looked out the window
Is that a familiar car?
Perhaps they aren't stopping here...
Ooops! They are!

Do Eyelets Serve A Greater Purpose?

Forgive me my kind scrapping friends
And one question let me pose...
Eyelets, tags and shakers
What are the purposes of those?

I have a trillion photos
That pose a looming task
And since I fail to know their use
I thought that I should ask...

I don't want to miss out on something
That I will regret later on
But seems to me that eyelets
On clothing should belong...

Years ago when I was sewing
And making baby clothes
I hammered and I pounded
A score or so of those.

And as for shaker boxes
Who invented those? (and why?)
I do not see the purpose
Although I really try!

If my purpose is my photo
To protect, preserve and show
Why do I need confetti...
I confess I do not know!

Labels, tags, brads and nail heads
I just cannot get hold
Of the newest and the trendiest—
It's gotten out of control!

What a great relief it was
And what a wonderful surprise
When we found our own special scrapping stuff
To replace sewing and office supplies.

But now it seems we're back again
To office supplies galore
Except the price is three times as much
At the local scrap booking store!

I'm really not complaining
But I really want to know
If they serve some greater purpose...
Will somebody let me know????

?

Labels, tags, brads and nail heads
I just cannot get hold
Of the newest and the trendiest--
It's gotten out of control!

A Cowlick

A cowlick is like a thumbprint
Except it's on your head
And unlike your thumbprint
It looks worse when
First you get out of bed!

You can brush it
You can comb it
But believe me when I say
That silly little cowlick
Will never go away!

Some people try to curl it
Or spray it till it's flat
While others try to hide it
Behind a great big hat.

But as for me I do not mind
The way it looks on me
It gives my hair a bit of sass
And per-son-ality!

A cowlick is like a thumbprint
Except it's on your head
And unlike your thumbprint
It looks worse when
First you get out of bed!

Plethora

I have a plethora of things to do
Some I've had a while and some are new...
My scraproom has an excess of ephemera
And a superfluity of clutter to wade through
With a profusion of page embellishments
Waiting for photo splits or glue!

The overflow of my cabinets
Lets the surplus trickle almost out the door
And the deluge of the plentiful
Lies in cluttered profusion on the floor.

While the abundance of artful objects
With which I can choose to play
Should brighten up my outlook
And add gladness to my day...

I stand perplexed amidst the land of plenty
And I feel the urge to take a nap
Perchance I'll dream how
To use all of these neat things––
Since I computer scrap...

?

I have a plethora of things to do
Some I've had a while and some are new...

143

INSPIRATIONAL

Everyone needs uplifting and inspirational thoughts to keep them going and to keep their faith strong. We all have down days—those "wish I could run away from home/work/ school days" when nothing seems to go right.

When I first started putting some of my most private thoughts into poetry, I kept them to myself, thinking they pertained only to me and that no one else would be interested. Then as I shyly began to share with friends, they often would ask me how I knew what they were going through.

I found that I could write, with God's guidance, the feelings that others were having as far as experiences that I've never had. I found I could write about divorce and remarriage and grand parenting and even for my friends with Downs Syndrome children as if I were in their shoes.

This helped me to understand that we all have heartaches and pains. We all have problems and trials and we all need someone to share with—the good and the bad. And we all need something to read that will encourage and inspire. Hopefully, you will find something here that will lift you up or help heal a hurting heart.

?

It is my hope and sincere prayer that you will find something in these pages to bring you, comfort if you are in pain, joy if you are sad and, stir your heart to long for a closer relationship with God. For that is truly the best gift one can ask for and the one gift available to all who seek it!

God's Hands

God's hands are all over the world
And no matter what people say
God's hands are visible
You see them every day.

God's hands are creamy white.
His hands are a golden tan.
His hands are darkest ebony
And rough from sea and sand.

His hands are soft and gentle
And his hands can be young or old.
His hands reach out in climates warm
Or in the coldest ice and snow.

You've seen His hands so many times
For God uses hands of those He loves
For things He needs hands to do!
If you've reached out to do His will...
Your hands are His hands too!

God Gave Us Hands

God gave us hands
And hearts and souls
And gave us His Spirit
So His Truth we would know.

God bid us His love to show
In everything our hands would do
And that our hearts
Would to Him be true.

From Your Friends

We pray for an angel to watch over you
To keep you safe and warm,
An angel sent from Heaven
To keep you safe from harm.

We pray for you encouragement
When you are feeling blue,
For friends with kind loving thoughts
To gently guide you through.

We ask for you sweet laughter
To come again to dwell
To heal that hurt inside your heart
That you know so well.

We pray that God will wrap you close
In His arms so loving and strong,
To let you feel His love for you
And know where you belong!

For you belong to He who created
The earth, the land and sea,
And He will keep his eyes on you
For all eternity

When you have trials and troubles
Lean on the Lord above
For He is able to give comfort
And fill your heart with love.

Prayer for Little One

God bless this little one
And restore him to perfect health I pray
And when comes morning's light again
Let him feel good enough to run and play!

Give him sweet gentle sleep tonight
And give his mommy peace
That your loving watch o'er this precious child
Will never ever cease.
Amen

God Bless You

God bless you and keep you
Safely through the night
And may He wake you gently
When comes the morning light.

May He fill your life with sunshine
And fill your heart with peace
And may your days bring happiness
And joys that will not cease.

IF

If you see me standing silently
And on my face you see a stare
Don't worry about me, dear friend
I'm just seeking God in prayer.

A Prayer

Father God in Heaven Above
Look down upon this child you love
And grant her peace throughout this night
And gently awake her with the morning's sweet light.

Let angels their sweet watch keep
Over this loved one as she sleeps
And guard her dreams that they may be
Restful and loving dreams from Thee.

Let her mind have the needed rest
And I pray that she will be blest
With love and hope and perfect peace
And that harassing fears would cease.

Let her feel your Presence
Throughout the stillness of the night
And let her know that all is well
That you make all things right.

We thank you Lord
For all you've done
And ask this Father
In the Name of The Son.
Amen

The older I get the more I realize
That everyone has tears and
everybody cries...

Wings of Angels

Wings of angels from above
Gently brush the ones I love
As they are watched
And kept safe from harm
Sheltered and from cold kept warm.

Heaven's gates will open wide
Welcoming those I love inside.
And there with God we will abide
With our loved ones side by side.

?

God-Parents

God made the moon
God made the sun.
And He created you
Precious little one.

Your parents chose me
To help guide you in His way
To listen your heart speak
And share your love each day.

I do not take it lightly
That they entrusted me
To share the joy of you dear one
And your God-Parent to be.

Nobody's Life Was Perfect

The older I get the more I realize
That everyone has tears and
everybody cries...
Everyone has had trials and everyone
has had pain
Some find it awful hard to get up and to
begin again.

Everyone has fears that try to haunt them
From things that hurt them long ago
The longer that I live on this earth
The more I know this
to be so.

Even when life seems at
its happiest
Most folks have baggage
from the past
That tries to interfere and pop up again
But we must dismiss those thoughts and fast.

When those phantoms of your childhood
try to haunt you
Dismiss them and send them away
For those shadows of your childhood
Have no right to your today.

The older I get the more I realize
That everyone has tears and
everybody cries...

Dreams

Sometimes our dreams are shattered
And for a time we are held down
With no room for smiles upon a face
That only wants to frown.

Sometimes tears seem to flow
At the mention of our dream
And life seems oh, so unfair
As if bursting at the seams.

But something good will come our way
Bestowed by God above
That will restore our joy and faith
And fill our hearts once more with love.

So dream your dreams if you want to dream
Dream of the best for you
For if you dare not to dream once more
How then can that dream come true?

?

Dare to Dream

If you want to dream
Dream larger than life
Dream of the best for you
For if you dare not to dream--
How then can your dreams come true?

Dream My Daughter

Today my daughter you dream
Of places you want to be
Of landmarks and palaces
Of things you want to see.

Tomorrow you will be older
And your dream will turn to a plan
You will plan to do a million things
And I'll be your biggest fan.

And soon you'll do so many things
I pray they will all be well worthwhile
But today I take pleasure in watching you
As you dream your dreams, my child.

Learning About the Game of Life

So many things he will learn from you
What to say and what to do
How to handle both joy and strife
And how to play honorably the
game of life...

Is Life a Game?

Some people say life is a game
And perhaps that could be true
I'm glad that if life is a game
I get to play my game with you!

Art of Life Graduate

Some people have stacks of degrees
And know facts and figures and such
And hold on to things that may seem important
But sometimes aren't worth too much...

They toss their expertise around
And frame their diplomas on the wall
But when you have a need for wisdom
They aren't the ones on whom you call...

Dad, you hold the prime example
Of the best of all degrees
That doesn't come from
A Department of Philosophy...

You have learned so much
About so many things
And graciously shared with us
Wonderful insights that you've gained...

Your thirst for knowledge
Has the admiration of us all
And is truly inspirational
And may I add that in your graduation cap...
You truly look sensational!!

Written for the father of my friend Morryann
Phillips upon the occasion of his graduation

Dad, you hold the prime example
Of the best of all degrees...

All I Want for Christmas

Father in Heaven up above
I know that you love the ones we love
And know the pain they're going through
And how helpless we feel as to what to do!
For Christmas I would ask you to bless
Each of my friends with happiness
With love and laughter that will never cease
But with each day only increase!

For those who have been feeling ill
I ask in accordance with your will
That you would heal their illness too
And all the thanks we'll give to you!
For those whose spirits need a touch
Who are feeling rather down today
We ask a touch from Your dear hand
To chase all despair and gloom away!

For those whose marriages might need
Your loving hand to intercede
This touch I ask for each and every one
Let their love be renewed and life be fun!
And for those with cares unspoken
Who are near despair
With hearts so broken...
We lift those friends up to You
And ask you to bless them through and through!

Father we know that the safest place on earth
Without you there would be the worst
But where you are and in your embrace
Becomes the worlds safest place!
No matter what the world may do
Lord, keep us hugged safe close to You!
In Jesus Name, Amen

If One Day

If when you awake one day
You find that I have been called away.
Do not fret or morn for me
And do not blame eternity!

Just smile when you think of me
And enjoy each pleasant memory
Of times long past and present fun
For my life has just begun.

When in God's presence I shall stand
I pray He takes me by my hand
And says "Welcome home my little one
Thank you for a job well done!"

What Was It Lord

What was it, Lord
That made you go
To Calvary so long ago
To give your life
On that cruel tree?
"Dear Child,"
He said, "It was for thee."

For One

God loves each person so very much
Each precious child born into this world
And He would still have sent His Son
For just one little boy or girl.

I Have This Day

I have this day to smell the roses
And feel the wind against my face
To bask in God's warm sunlight
And to feel my family's sweet embrace.

I have this day to view the ocean
And stand upon the shore
To ponder all the mysteries
That eternity has in store.

I do not take it lightly
And always when I pray
I thank the Lord in Heaven
That I have this day!

And when the day is over
And the sun indeed has set
I thank Him for the morning
That I have not seen as yet.

And if I should rise upon the morrow
And have yet another day
Then it is just another blessing
That the Good Lord sent my way.

Father,
Let Me Always Be Mindful to Say
Thank You Lord That
I Have This Day.

Isn't It Amazing?

I watched a butterfly pause on a flower
And I felt such a reverence for God
And His almighty power.

So awesome, powerful and mighty is He
But He created a delicate butterfly
and the honeybee!

I watched the sunshine go behind the clouds
And I heard the thunder roar
But I was not frightened of my God
I only loved Him more.

For a great and mighty Lord is He
But He provides shelter from
Storms for you and me
Oh, how amazing my God can be!

?

With joy in my heart
I celebrate this day with you
And always will be here for you
Wherever you are and whatever you do.

Confirmation Day or Baptism

May joy and happiness fill your heart
And may this day set you apart
With honor to our God above
May you feel His presence and His love.

On this day as you seek to grow
And more about your God to know
May you hear His voice as He speaks to you
And to His commandments always be true.

And may you receive His blessings
In such a way
To add unlimited joy
On this special day.

Celebrating Confirmation or Baptism

With joy in my heart
I celebrate this day with you
And always will be here for you
Wherever you are and whatever you do.

God loves you and cherishes you
For you are a treasure
His love for you exceeds
Anything that can be measured.

And this day is an answered prayer
That this moment in your life I could share.
May God Bless You on this Special Day
And send Peace, Love and Joy Your Way.

Easter Baptism

What a wonderful Easter Day
I know God hears every prayer I pray
For here you are honoring the Father and Son
By being baptized, my little one!

In my heart I have such joy
Over seeing the choice you made today
Such joy that could not be expressed
By any words that I might say.

But I've stored in a very special place
The awesome memories of this day
And be assured that for the rest of my life
They will be treasured and replayed.

Watching God's World

I sit here in my window
And look out upon the scene
Nobody pays much attention
I'm such a tiny human being.
Mommy thinks I'm watching
All the cars go passing by
(She doesn't realize that
I'm looking at God's sky!).
Daddy thinks I'm looking at the trucks
With monster wheel and frame
(He didn't see the butterfly
or notice when it came).
I watch it all throughout the day
From my tiny baby seat.
And being so fresh sent from God
The world looks oh so sweet!

159

Almost Home

He had been traveling quite a bit
And seemed so frequently away from home
But at each stopover or destination
He would call me on the phone
And say with anticipation
"Hey Sweetheart! I'm almost home!"
Even the puppy dogs were excited
When they saw me smiling and gay
Knowing that when Mom is happy
Daddy must be on his way!
Oh, how I wish for every traveler
That in this whole world might roam
They would know the precious sweetness
Of someone joyously exclaiming
"My loved one is almost home!"

?

I cannot help but compare our travels here
To the journey from this earth
Where I have my earthly family
And where I was given birth,
To the journey that takes a lifetime
To reach God's Heavenly Throne
And as the years pass quickly by
I feel I'm almost Home!
There is no need to call ahead
I speak to God each day
He knows every thought I have
And every word I say.
And I hope He looks out through Heaven's portals
Wearing the biggest Heavenly grin
Swings those Pearly Gates open wide
And says "Welcome, Thena, Come Right In!"

Poverty

I saw houses if you call them such
Made of pieces of wood and tin
And nothing much...
I saw one, then many more
With very thin walls and shaky doors
And I doubt if any of them had floors...
I saw houses that made me cry
Why these people...
Why not I?
But I saw people in each one
That loved and laughed
And even had fun...
I saw people who accepted life's lot
And said, "I'm thankful
For the things I've got..."
I saw people with hearts and souls
I saw people in extreme poverty
Who were just people like you and me.
I saw people that God loves too.
Just as He loves me and He loves you
I saw people...
I saw people in a brand new light
Who needed no frills
To provide delight.
God help me to see people everyday
In a kind and loving way
And let the words that I may say
And the acts that I do
Always reflect my love for You.

The Heart Doesn't Speak In Fancy Words

The heart doesn't speak in fancy words
That only learned men can understand
But speaks in soft and gentle sighs
And touches of the hand...

The heart speaks in glances sweet and loving
And tender gentle kisses
It speaks in such subtle ways
That sometimes their voice a person misses...

The heart speaks in gentle thoughts
That cause a loving act
A gentle touch upon the head
Or a pat upon the back.
Poets through the ages
From the dawn of man
With their pen have expounded on the feelings
Instilled by the simplest touch of the human hand.

The tiniest baby knows of love
And needs not the poet's word
For he is shown the power of love
By every special tender act
And each loving coo he's heard.

For those whose tongues cannot express
In eloquent poetry or stylish prose
Their love song for our Lord above
He sees your heart and knows.

He sees your love for friend and spouse
And child loved tenderly and sweetly
And will give you the words to say
To share your heart with them completely.

For He who created heart and soul
And body mind and spirit
Has given us a voice with which to speak
And provided listening ears to hear it.

Your Voice

O Lord, You spoke to me today
In such an un-dramatic way
I almost missed Your voice so still
That urged me on to do Your will.

There was Your voice
Inside my head
How gentle were
The words You said.

"Only as your foot
Goes into the water
Will the waves begin to part
Don't hesitate or wait
Now's the time to start."

Lord, help me to always recognize
Your voice so sweet and still
Guide me every day, Dear Lord
And keep me in Your will.

What is the greatest gift
you ever received?
Mine was given to me
When I first believed.

God gave me this poem in the form of a song...

I was in my thirties when my beloved mother died from a stroke. I missed her so much and sought comfort one night as I shed tears of sorrow. God gave me this poem on the next page in the form of a song (since I'm no great singer, I assume it was to help me remember it long enough to write it down). As I wrote it, I realized this is not only what I would say to my daughter but also what my mom would say to me. Even as it comforted me, through the years others have told me that it brought comfort to them as well.

I cried so hard and wept so much
That I could not speak or see--
Until I felt His touch upon my head--
And heard, "YOUR MOTHER IS WITH ME!"

?

If my Savior should call me home
I will not stop or hesitate.
And if I should get there first
I'll wait for you by the Pearly Gates!

164

Going Home

If my Savior should call me home
Do not be sad that I must go.
For all I do and all I am
Is because I love Him so.
If my Savior should call me
To come to Him in Heaven above
I will not hesitate to go
I must leave behind the ones I love.
But do not weep for me
Or mourn the fact that I am gone.
Just think of me as being home
Where I belong!
If my savior should call me
I will gladly go.
Do not use heroic means
To keep me here below.
I'll be sad to cause you pain
If my leaving should cause you such,
But I'll rejoice when I hear His voice
And His garment I can touch.
Don't say "How sad that she is gone."
Or cry or mourn for me
Just picture me with a smiling face
Seated at Jesus' knee.
If any cross words or deeds
Between us should ever pass
Be assured they were forgotten
As soon as they were past.
I want "no regrets" or "I should have done's"
To follow me when I leave.
There's no reason for "I wish I had's."
I want no one to grieve.
If my Savior should call me home
I will not stop or hesitate.
And if I should get there first
I'll wait for you by the Pearly Gates!

165

From a Dear Friend...

Read It Again!

I picked up my Grandmother's Bible
When she went home to Glory.
That old book was so precious to her
As it told of her Savior's story.

Its cover was worn and faded with time
But the messages held in its pages
Were well imprinted on Grandmother's heart,
It had been her guide through the ages.

As I thumbed through this book I shall never forget
The words that she printed therein;
At the end of each Testament,
The Old and the New,
In large letter she wrote: "Read it again!"

"Read it again," my Grandmother wrote
In that wonderful book of old.
The wisdom I find in those few little words
Are to me far more precious than gold!
—Shirley Jamison Stockel ©
Used with permission

*One of my very dearest friends shared this poem with
me several years ago and it has stayed in my heart
and mind. My heartfelt thanks to her for giving me
permission to share it with you. She had wonderful
parents and grandparents whose love of God helped
mold her into the wonderful woman she is today.*

Truly Amazing

I look at the beauty that surrounds us
In the simplest of things
The beauty of a butterfly
Or a sparkling stream.

I see wonder in the eyes
Of a child at play
And feel the thrill when hearing
Loving words that people say.

Awesome wonders meet my eyes
In so many things I see
But I find it wonderfully amazing
Just how much God loves you and me!

?

Awesome wonders meet my eyes
In so many things I see
But I find it wonderfully amazing
Just how much God loves you and me!

LITTLE BOYS

I don't have any little boys of my own but I grew up with two older brothers. I take examples from our childhood and from observing the sons of my friends and family members and use those to create my verses about little boys.

I 'remember on paper' some of the adventures and escapades that involved my brothers. I admired them, followed them, mimicked them and at times (when I had been meddling in their possessions) I feared them but I always loved them!

They taught me many valuable lessons and I think I taught them a few. They teased me unmercifully but would protect me from any bully that would dare try to do the same.

They checked up on me when I was older and because of their wisdom handed down, I was able to function better as a high school and college student. Boys are wonderful, especially when they grow up to be big brothers!!

My Rainbow

When I see the rainbow
I don't look for the pot of gold
For you are my rainbow boy
That I can have and hold!
When I wish for the rain to stop
And for the sun again to shine
I look forward to the rainbow
Little rainbow boy of mine!

Boy Rhymes With Joy

A baby is a blessing
Sent by God above
Bundled up in sunbeams
To fill our hearts with love.

But babies all grow bigger
And soon are babes no more
But those who have been there
Know there is more joy in store.

For a boy is a blessing
When he becomes a lad
Big enough and strong enough
To follow around with Dad!

He is a source of inspiration
When he begins to ask
Lots of leading questions
About your daily tasks!

He is an amazing mixture
Of love, motion and zest
And when he's unpredictable
Is when you love him best!

There's just no telling
What he will do and say
The only thing you know for sure
Is that you love him more each day!

Yes, babies are a blessing
That God sent us to enjoy
But there is a reason
Why Boy rhymes with JOY!

Two Tiny Feet

Two tiny feet
Precious as can be
Taking that first step
To come to me!

Two little feet
In his baby shoes
Running to his mommy
Chasing away my blues!

Two little feet in rain boots
Splashing in a puddle
Running to his mommy
For a warming snuggle!

Two teenage feet
Dressing for a date
Wearing the latest fashion...
Don't be out late!

In shoes all shined and bright
He watches his bride walk down the aisle
He gazes at her so lovingly
And I see his happy smile.

Together they walk down the aisle
And through the door as man and wife
Taking those first steps
Into their brand new life.

Does he know that in my heart
These steps he takes today
Remind me of those precious steps
When he first walked my way?

The Two of You

Today I watched you with our son...
The two of you so sweetly at play
And I know that your love for each other
Grows dearer every day.

And in your eyes I see your love
Reflected as if your eyes would glow
You have always been my hero
And today, more than you'll ever know.

I see the trust in his innocent face
And the wonderment he's feeling
He is so content to be sitting with you
Just thinking, looking and being.

Thank you sweetheart for loving me
And for loving our child as you do
And now tears are streaming from my face
I'm so filled with love for you!

?

Today I watched you with our son...
The two of you so sweetly at play
And I know that your love for each other
Grows dearer every day.

For A Moment

For a moment I held you
When you were born
And you nestled down
All snug in my arms
And life was dream like...

For a moment you were a toddler
And you played on a trike
Soon you were learning
How to ride a real bike
And life was exhilarating
As I watched you learn—
For a moment...

Then you were a teenager
Aching to be free
We had long discussions
Just you and me
And sometimes we agreed
To disagree—
For a moment...

Now we share a dance together
On this your wedding day
Soon you will join your lovely bride
And will whisk her away.

And soon you will be the head
Of a family of your own
And all of these memories
Will be replaced with special moments of your own.

All of these moments
So fleeting and fast
Came so lovingly
And then they were past...

Oh God help us to notice and realize
How precious these moments
As each one flies by.

And give us a nudge
That we recognize each day
All those precious moments
That you send our way!

?

Is anything cuter
Than ten tiny toes
Maybe little baby ears
Or a button nose
Or two little feet
So chubby and cute
Or a round little body
In it's birthday suit?

All American Boy

You are such a wonder.
You bring me unequaled joy.
You are my little miracle
My all American boy!

You like frogs and tadpoles
And you think dirt is fine.
You are happy in the grass and dirt
And you are a friend to grime!

You find happiness in the snow.
You think storms are fun.
You don't mind the rain at all,
My all American son!

Your pockets are never empty.
Your feet are never still.
You sometimes are a bit stubborn
I'd say you are strong willed.

I count my blessings when
the sun is setting low
With a happy heart filled with love and joy
And the first blessing that I count
Is my all American Boy!

You are my Little Miracle
My all American Boy!

174

Boy Rhymes With Joy
(Version two)

Boy rhymes with ploy
Sometimes they will annoy
A girl may be coy
But never so a boy!

A boy may drive you crazy
May sometimes appear lazy
But let him bring a daisy
And your heart will turn to mush!

Never look in pockets
Unless your heart is strong
Cause there may be a frog, rat, or lizard there...
My list could go on...

But like a ray of sunshine
On a cloudy day
The antics of little boys
Are treasured in every way!

?

But like a ray of sunshine
On a cloudy day
The antics of little boys
Are treasured in every way!

Only God Could Create a Little Boy

Look at that wonderful creature
That we call a little boy
Only God in Heaven above
Could create such a package of joy!

Who would have thought of all of the things
That occupy a little boys mind?
If we were to look inside his head
What wonderful things would we find?

His imagination when let run free
Lets him wondrous things to see
And he finds joy in all manner of things
From rocket ships to tennis shoestrings!

He can love a puppy dog or a rat
With just as much ease
And when given the opportunity
A little boy loves to please.

Human beings can create
All manner of things to bring joy
But only a wonderful God of love
Could have created a little boy!

Five Boys!

Look at them, five boys in a row
How did I ever arrive
At this magic number
I really don't even know

Five boys as babes
Born from my womb
And set up with cribs
In tiny little rooms

Five times of watching
Each one as they grew
And welcoming the next one
And loving him too!

Five times the turmoil
And five times the fun
And as I watch them mature and grow
I know the best is yet to come!

Boys Into Men

What a wonderful way
For God to begin
The end product
That we call MEN!

Our little boys
Start out so small
But love rough and tumble
And don't mind a fall!

They love to climb trees
And flex imaginary muscles
And to keep up with them
You have to hustle!

But what a wonderful thrill
When childhood suddenly ends
And all of a sudden
Our boys have become MEN!

At Play with Bugs and More...

Dying Easter Eggs

Today is such a special day
I've waited all year through
To get to dye my Easter eggs
In pink and green and blue!

When Mommy takes the colors out
And places them on the table
I'd love to dye a zillion eggs
But I'm just not able!

So I dye the most I can
And Mommy does the rest
All our eggs look beautiful
But I love blue ones the best!

The blue reminds me of the sky
The pink is cotton candy
The green is like the spring time grass
(For hiding eggs that's handy!)

I love to hunt the Easter eggs
And eating them is fun
I know that when we dye our eggs
Springtime has just begun!

Carries Version of Dying Easter Eggs

Today is such a special day
I've waited all year through
To get to dye my Easter eggs
In pink and green and blue!

178

When Mommy takes the colors out
And places them on the table
I'd love to dye a zillion eggs
But I'm just not able!

So since I can't dye every egg
I do what I am able.
I dye some eggs, the floor,
My clothes, my brother and the kitchen table.

Mommy tries to make such pretty eggs.
To see patterns when we look.
But I think the eggs look better,
With the colors all gobbley-gook!

My brother and I love it so,
We giggle and ask for more.
It's so neat to see colored eggs
Fall onto Mommy's floor.

We love this time so very much.
We don't understand why,
Just when our eggs AND clothes are colorful
That's when Mom yells GOODBYE!

She yanks us out of the kitchen
And plops us in the tub.
She swears about a lawsuit
If out the colors will not scrub.

But I think Mommy really likes it too,
She just forgets it for a while.
But she'll remember the fun we had,
From the pictures of our smiles.
Written by Carrie Heisler

Little Ketchup Face

Some folks don't realize
That ketchup is for more than fries.
You can put it on anything
When you want to add some 'zing'!

I love it on all kinds of stuff
Just can't seem to get enough
And fortunately find no disgrace...
In having ketchup on
My FACE!!

?

Bugs

Moms don't always understand
Why a bug seems to be in demand
To a boy who loves to run and play
And gather little bugs throughout the day.

To Mom a bug is yucky stuff
And she just isn't tough enough
To hold or cradle a bug in hand
Like her adorable little man.
For be it a firefly, beetle or ladybug
I've found you just can't hug...
a bug.

I Love Worms

Mommy doesn't understand
My love for bugs and worms.
Whenever I bring home a "friend"
My mommy shudders and squirms!

Worms are such a wonderful pets
That never run away.
You find them in a nice pail of earth
And there the worms will stay!

A butterfly will fly away
And has to be out and free,
But when I find a big ole worm
He has to stay with me!

I put them in my pockets
And take them around with me
To show them all the places
I think a worm would like to see!

I'd like to show the worms my room
And keep them in with me
But as for now, I'm sad to say
My mommy doesn't agree!

?

Some things never change
Down through the years
Little boys love creepy crawly things
That a mommy sometimes fears...

A Little Dirt Can't Hurt

I don't know why people say
"Don't get dirty"
When I go out to play.
I know from several years of fun
That no matter what our parents say
A little dirt can't hurt!

So if I'm working in the yard
Or when I'm playing really hard.
I wish that parents would understand
That boys and dirt go hand in hand!!

Fortunate is the Boy With a Tree

How fortunate is the little boy
Whose yard holds a tree
He is the most fortunate boy
That there ever could be.

For a tree will hold a nest of robins
In its branch up so high
And a boy can climb its branches
To reach up and touch the sky.

A tree can hold a swing of wood
With ropes so it can fly
And in that swing a little boy
Many hours can pass by.

And moms can watch this wonderful sight
And remember when they were young
And loved to swing in a wooden swing
And have hours and hours of fun!

Superboy!

Look at him in his superman cape!
Look how cute my son is
All the super powers of the world
He now believes are his!

He holds out his hands and parts the sky
Making room for the wind to blow
He tilts his head and lowers his sights
To focus on the stars below!

His cape flows out from behind him
As he soars so fast and free
He is a super duper hero
And he belongs to me!

Brandon Running From the Wave

In my heart in a special place
Are sweet memories to save
I put a new one there today....
Brandon running from a wave!

What fun, delight and pure joy
Were in the eyes of this dear boy
As he ran and laughed in glee
What a wonderful sight to see!

I know he will do wonderful things
And those will be tenderly tucked away
But the newest treasure in my heart
Is Brandon running from the wave today...
Written for my friend Martha Crowther

Backyard Joy

Look at him standing there
Sun kissed skin and water soaked hair!
Look at him and his muscle man pose
And as for muscles, look at the size of those!

Look at that face and puckered up lips
Look at that tummy and tiny little hips!
You are looking at my backyard joy
My adorable wonderful little boy!

A Boy Needs A Very Best Friend

A boy needs a very best friend
A confidant, and a loyal buddy
A partner with whom he can climb a tree
Or play in the puddles and get muddy!

A boy needs a special kind of pal
One who likes to ride bikes and scooters
But one who can play on a Gameboy
And knows his way 'round computers!

A boy needs a friend to be silly with
And who loves each bug and each critter
One who will play out late in the dark
And a pal who isn't a quitter!

Every boy needs a special friend
And to find one is special indeed.
I'm so happy that you have such a friend—
Exactly the friend that you need!

184

Cowboy Ditties and Boo Boo's

A cowboy's work is never done
We wake up before the sun.
We work so hard during the day
That we get rowdy when we play!

There must be angels
Especially assigned
To watch over every cowboy––
I know I have mine!

?

I want to be a cowboy
When I am all grown up.
I will have a big ole horse
And a trusty pup!

I'll join a cowboy group
And together we will ride
In rodeos and cattle drives
Together side by side!

We will round up cattle
And will all have time to play
When we meet in the bunkhouse
At the end of our cowpoke day!

?

I'm a cowpoke
Just look and see
How a cowpoke
Is supposed to be!
Got my vest
Got my chaps
Do I have a horse?
Perhaps....

185

Band-Aid

When I fall and scrape my knee
My mommy puts a band-aid on me!
Knee or leg or face or chin
My mommy puts a band-aid on them!

If I have a tummy ache
In the middle of the night
Mommy comes into my room
Even if there is no light!

She brings me stuff to make it stop
The hurting that I feel inside
And she knows that I feel better
After I have cried.

If I have a bad day at school
And I just need to talk.
My mommy gets her sweater on
And we go for a walk.

When I have had an awful day
Or hurt myself while I played
My Mommy and her hugs and kisses
Are better than the best Band-Aid!

?

When I fall and scrape my knee
My mommy puts a band-aid on me!
Knee or leg or face or chin
My mommy puts a band-aid on them!

My Knees

Sometimes during a fun day
I scrape my knees while I'm at play
Even when they're black and blue
My mom knows just what to do.

Sometimes if I've fallen really hard
A dose of medicine might be required
But usually it's just a scratch I've taken
And my body is just a wee bit shaken.

When Mom comes and cleans up my knee
She gives a hug and kiss to me.
I don't mind the kiss at all—
It's kind of nice when you've had a fall!

Bed Time

Big Boy Bed

Today was a special day
It was a landmark in my book
I got a special big boy bed
Oh come and take a look!

No more baby crib for me!
I'm a big boy now!
I can get in and out all by myself
No one needs to show me how!

I am so happy to have my bed
It's one I will want to keep
It is like the one that Mommy has
Where she and Daddy sleep!

187

LITTLE GIRLS

What is more precious than a little girl? As the mom of a daughter I loved every single moment of having a little girl in the house. From the moment of her first gurgle and coo, she could wrap everyone in the household around her little finger. Come to think of it, she still can, many years later!

I was so excited and blessed to have a baby girl to love and cuddle, to dress up in frills and ruffles and to teach and sometimes overprotect! And little girls really do grow up in such a delightful way!

Little girls bring something special to a household. And once they arrive, your world is never the same.

?

Pretty As a Picture

Pretty as a picture
Lovely as a doll
Please don't grow too fast
Stay little for a while!

Dress in lace and ribbons
For a few minutes more
You are our little angel
That we've always waited for!

All American Girl

She's our all American Girl
Dainty as a flower in her frilly dress
But a mighty slugger in her uniform—
One of little league's best!

She's not your average girl
She can hit and she can run
Better than most boys on the team
And she will do it all in fun!

She loves to play out in the dirt
And is comfortable in the mud
As long as when she comes inside
There are bubbles in her tub!

She is soft and she is feminine
A lovely sight to see
She's a little American beauty
And she belongs to me!!

She is such a joy to us
And I know the day will come,
When this little American beauty
Will be a grown up one!

She is such a joy to us
And I know the day will come
When this little American beauty
Will be a grown up one!

Outdoor Girl

She's an outdoor girl!
Look at that face
Tanned and lovely
From the wind's embrace!

She's an outdoor girl
Look at those eyes
Brighter and clearer
Than the morning sky!

She's an outdoor girl
Full of joy and fun
She is a bundle of loving energy
Kissed by the sun!

Moonbeams on Your Face

I stand in awe and look at you
With the moonlight on your face.
The soft and gentle moonbeams
Like the sweetest of embrace.
I see your eyes stare upward
As the fullness of the moon you see
And I thank the Heavenly Father
For His precious gift to me!
I can't promise you the moon
Or all the stars that shine
But I can promise I will love you forever
Dearest child of mine!

Little Sweetheart

You are so sweet
And tiny and new
Everything is so
Perfect about you.

I look in awe
And tears try to fall
As I am overwhelmed
With the joy of it all.

So, I kiss you
Gently on your tiny head
And place you lovingly
Back in your bed.

But my heart is filled
Up to the top
With a love for you
That will never stop.

?

You are so sweet
And tiny and new
Everything is so
Perfect about you.

My Daughter

You are my child, my daughter
My precious little girl
And I love you more, my little one
Than anything in this world.

How could I be so blessed
As to receive a gift like you
It only goes to prove
Dreams really do come true!

I dream big dreams for you
Though you are so young now
But I know that big dreams come true
Even though we don't know how.

I dream of a life that is full of joy
And a life that is fun to live.
I dream for you a heart full of love
One that is quick to forgive.

Oh, little one my heart is so full
Of love and dreams and such
That to be sure that you aren't just a dream
I have to reach out and touch!

As for my dreams for you, precious one
I know they will all come true
For the biggest dream I ever could have dreamed
Was the dream I dreamed of you!

You are My Child, My Daughter
My Precious Little Girl...

My Little Daughter's First Bath

So innocent pure and sweet
Little love that makes life complete
Unclothed to the naked eye of yours and mine
But wrapped in Heaven's love Divine.

I place you now in your little tub
And caress your precious baby skin
Stopping as I give you your first bath
To give kisses now and then.

How I love that baby skin
So soft and sweet to mommy's touch
Precious little baby girl
Your parents love you so very much!

?

Pouffy Dress

I'm my grandmother's little angel
The apple of her eye
Angels blow me kisses
From the fluffy clouds up in the sky.

The sunbeams dance across my hair
And the wind poufs up my dress
And all the while I feel God's love
And know that I've been blessed.

For A Moment (Baby to Bride)

For a moment I held you
When you were born
And you nestled down
All snug in my arms
And life was dream like—
For a moment...

For a moment you were a toddler
And you played on a trike
Soon you were learning
How to ride a real bike
And life was exhilarating
As I watched you learn—
For a moment...

Then you were a teenager
Aching to be free
We had long discussions
Just you and me
And sometimes we agreed
To disagree—
For a moment...

Now I watch you walk down the aisle
Moving toward your sweetheart
I see you smile
For a moment...

All of these moments
So fleeting and fast
Came so lovingly
And then they were past...

Oh God help us to notice and realize
How precious these moments
As each one flies by...

And give us a nudge
That we recognize each day
All those precious moments
That you send our way!

Princess of Everything!

With a pretty dress
And lovely bow in my hair
I like to dress like a princess
When I go anywhere.

My lovely room is my castle
And my parents are queen and king.
With my dolly always at my side,
I'm Princess of Everything!

I'd love to be like Cinderella
And go to the ball some night
Or visit with those little folks
Like the beautiful Snow White.

A princess has a lovely life
And her job is to be sweet
Acting in a princess like way
To every one she meets!

I treat my dolly kindly
And never fuss or scold her
She is content to have
A princess mom to hold her.

Daughters

Daughters are always loved
In such a special way.
Parents remember every thing they do
And every thing that say.

Daughters have a special way
Of lighting up a room,
Their very presence in our lives
Chases away the threat of gloom.

That's why for them a parent
Sends Heaven ward each day
Fervent prayers for all good things
To come their daughter's way!

Ponytail Princess

Today in love and humble awe
I smiled at the sweetness that I saw.
My angel in her little chair
With her first ponytail
In her baby hair.

Oh how my mommy's heart did beat
At seeing such a precious treat.
Oh tiny one I love you so
You will live and laugh and grow
But in my mind I will treasure today
When you wore a ponytail out to play!

Little Ballerina

My darling little baby girl
With sparkling eyes of blue
How I love the sweetness
Of everything that's you.

Little ballerina in a tutu
Dancing in our world
Lovely, dainty delicate
Our fair-haired little girl!

Our precious little ballerina
Dancing as we played her song
Lovely little angel
With only one thing wrong...

On her tiny little toes
Which ballet slippers should adore
Her favorite tall red leather boots
Our ballerina wore!!

Our Little Ballerina

Little ballerina in a tutu
Dancing in our world
Lovely, dainty and delicate
Our fair-haired little girl!
Our precious little ballerina
Dancing as we played her song
Lovely little angel
Smiling as gracefully she dances on.
So poised and confident
Dancing for all the world to see
You can dance happily and free from worry
When you are only three!!

Little Girls with Cooper Colored Hair

Copper colored hair on little girls
Reflecting sunlight on dainty little curls
Reminds me of the golden days
Of childhood once again
With curls kissed by the sunlight
And embraced lovingly by the wind...

Daddy's Little Girl

You are your daddy's little girl
You fill my day with joy
I love the way you smile and giggle
At the things that you enjoy!

I love the way you tilt you head
And your chubby baby cheeks
I love the way your eyes light up
When your mommy speaks!

You are our little angel
A bundle full of love
A miracle in denim
Created by God above!

You are flowers in the garden
You are sunshine in the spring
You are happiness in ponytails
You are our everything!

You are the center of our world
And we thank the Lord above
Each day for sending us
Such a wonderful child to love!

Daddy's Little Angel

She's Daddy's little angel
His sweetheart little girl
She's the rainbow in his cloudy day
She's his diamond, she's his pearl.

She is an angel sent from Heaven
To brighten up his day
She was sent to be his sunshine
Giving hugs and kisses all the way!

She can wrap him around her finger
She is everything worthwhile
She stole his heart completely
And she did it with her smile.

Daddy's Little Angels

They are Daddy's little angels
His sweetheart little girls
They're the rainbows in his cloudy day
They're his diamonds, they're his pearls.

They are angels sent from Heaven
To brighten up his day
God sent them to be his sunshine
Giving hugs and kisses all the way!

They can wrap him around their fingers
They are everything worthwhile
They stole his heart completely
And they each did it with a smile.

Only God Could Create a Little Girl

Look at that wonderful blessing
That we call a little girl
Only God in Heaven above
Could create such a little parcel of love!

Who would have thought of all the sweet things
That having a little girl would bring
What wonderful pictures would we find
If we could only glimpse into her mind?

She plays with her dollies
And babies them so
Just like her mommy
With her face all aglow.

She rocks her dolly
To sleep each night
And in bed her sleeping arms
Hold her baby so tight.

She can love a puppy dog
Or adore a kitty cat
But squeals in disgust
At the sight of a rat!

Human beings can create
All manner of things to bring joy
But only a wonderful God of love
Could have created a little girl
For us to love!

Look at that Wonderful Blessing
That we call a Little Girl...

Daughters Are God's Gift (Baby Girl)

God creates a special gift
In His Heaven above
A gift that is full of joy and laughter
Full of sunshine and of love.

He places all of these wonderful things
Along with a tender heart
Inside a tiny baby girl
And blesses each precious part.

He gives her tiny rosebud lips
And the softest baby skin
And just when she seems perfect
He touches her once again.

Then He sends her to her family
Through her earthly mom to be
And she blesses all who love her
For all eternity!

I know the Father does these things
That only He could do
For there is no other way to explain
A blessing such as you!

God creates a special gift
In His Heaven above
A gift that is full of joy and laughter
Full of sunshine and of love.

I Love to Dress Up!

I love pretty dresses
And shoes to match my dress.
I love to wear panty hose
And look my very best!

I love to polish my nails
And give my hair a twirl
Guess that is why
I enjoy being a girl!

Playing Dress Up

Playing in mommy's clothes
Is such fun to do
I like to pretend I'm her
And that I'm a mommy too!

I like to try on her dresses
And I love to wear her shoes
And Mommy doesn't mind at all
In fact she lets me choose!

Well Heeled

Dressing up in Mommy's heels
Oh how very good it feels!

I love to try on her pretty hats
High-heeled boots or sporty flats!

I love the clothes that Mommy loves
From casual chic to dressy gloves!

In Mommy's Shoes

Look at me in Mommy's shoes
I look so very grown
I think that I will keep them on
'Til everyone I've shown!

I can't wait until Daddy comes home
And I can greet him at the door
For although he sees me every day
He hasn't seen me in heels before!

What Fun to Dress Up

What fun to dress up
And be something new
What fun to be someone
Who's not really you!

What fun to be a tiger
And growl at the world
Or to be a princess
Instead of a regular girl!

I can be a scarecrow
And shoo away birds in flight
By waving my straw arms at them
And giving them quite a fright!

What fun to go around
In the neighborhood and show
My funny costumes
To the people I know!

203

Little Ballerinas

Tiny little feet
Precious as can be
In soft satin slippers
Dancing just for me.

Little ballerinas in their tutus
Oh this is too much fun.
They dance like little angels
Each and every one!

Dance On

Dance on beautiful child
And breathe in beauty and grace
Just look at the sparkle in your eyes
Just look at that lovely face.

Dance on with strength of body and mind
And let your spirit soar
Dance on until your find your dream
And then dance on some more.

We watch you dance and applaud you
For your joy is so sweet to see
Dance on and enjoy the dance
For it was truly meant to be.

Tiny little feet
Precious as can be
In soft satin slippers
Dancing just for me.

The Dance

The dance is lovely
And you look so sweet
You move so gracefully
On such delicate feet.

Your dance is lively
And full of fun
You light up the room
Like a dainty little sun.

You move so expertly
No matter which dance you choose
Your feet are like instruments
Cushioned in dainty shoes.

How beautiful you are
And how talented and sweet
Whether dancing the ballet
Or to a Latin beat!

Wave Dancer

Look at her standing there
Waiting for the waves to come
Daintily she steps into
The first....
Then second one.

Finally lost in her own world
She becomes our dancing girl.
Dancing with her head held high
As if hearing music from the sky
She is our
Wave Dancer....

Little Girl in Pigtails Poem

Look at you
Sitting there
Pigtails so cute
Sticking up in the air!

Look at my princess
In overalls of denim
They are so adorable
Since you are in them!

Oh aren't you a sweetie pie
And Mom's little cutie--
Someday my denim princess
I know you will be
An all American beauty!

Little Girls in Curls

Oh how sweet are little girls
With their adorable little curls!
Some with natural curls are blessed
And always seem to look their best.

While others need the helping hand
Of wrapping each curl in a strand
And wear curlers in their hair if they
Want their lovely curls to stay!

But fortunately some believe it's fun
To wear their curlers out in the sun
And know they will be beautifully coiffed
Before the day is done!

Little Girl Shadow

Looking out the window
Is a precious little one
Behind her is the shadow
Cast by the summer sun.
I can't help but think
As your photograph I see
That the shadow represents
The child you used to be.
The serious look on your sweet face
Makes me wonder if you know
That only today will you be this young
That you will surely grow.
Sweet little child enjoy this carefree time
And laugh and play in the sun
For it will be soon enough to know
Of the woman you will become!

Monster in My Closet

There was a monster in my closet
I saw it just last night
It reared its ugly monster head
When Mommy turned out the light!
There was a monster in my closet
But it's not there today
When Daddy came into my room
The monster ran away!
Monsters are afraid of Daddies
Guess it's cause Daddies are big and strong
They look right at monsters
And send them back where they belong!!

My Favorite Pumpkin

You are my favorite pumpkin!
You are the cutest in the patch.
I love your little pumpkin nose
And pumpkin eyes that match!

I love your cute pumpkin smile,
And your little pumpkin frame
Your teeny tiny pumpkin toes
And your sweet pumpkin name!

Yes, you're my favorite pumpkin
The cutest I could ever hope to see
And I will tell everyone that I meet
That the cutest pumpkin belongs to me!

Men in Her Life

The men in her life
Are older by far
Are they smitten with her?
Yes, they are.

The men in her life adore her
And smile when they see her face
They shower her with hugs and kisses
And a sweet and gentle embrace.

The men in her life will be always
At her beck and call every day
They won't ever tire of her
And won't ever leave her and go away.

She has known them forever
And they loved her right from the start
For one she calls Dad and the other Grandpa
And she stole each of their hearts.

My Daddy

I love my Daddy
He is so wonderful to me
He lifts me up on his shoulders
When I need to be taller to see!

I love my Grandpa
He just can't be beat
In knowing exactly
How to make my day complete!

Mommy's Girls

Three little girls in the garden
Looking for Easter eggs in the tree
Laughing and giggling and having fun
And these lovelies belong to me!

Three little girls in the sunshine
Playing and having fun
There is no bigger blessing
Not a single one.

Children having fun together
Healthy and happy and free
Are the most wonderful gift
That God could give to me!

Thank you Lord for the sunshine
Thank you Lord for each tree
But thanks most of all for the
wonderful children
That you so lovingly gave to me!

My Baby Lost Her First Tooth Today

My baby lost her first tooth today
I knew eventually
I'd have to say
My baby lost a tooth today.

I knew that she would grow up
Like every kid (or every pup)
And couldn't stay my baby
But I thought that maybe...

It would still be a little while
That she would be a tiny child
And I would have a bit more time
With this little one of mine...

But I see the signs so fast they come
And this is just the very first one
Childhood will soon be gone away
And my baby lost her first tooth today...

?

Ms. Tooth Fairy I watched for you
But I got so sleepy that I feel asleep
But I so wanted to find out
Just what you do-
With all those teeth you keep.

Tooth Fairy Poems

Don't worry about your tooth
I will keep it safe and sound
The best way to pay you for it
Is with this (dollar) I've found.

I bet you wonder
Just what I do with tiny teeth
From little boys and girls
To me they look like jewels—
Like tiny little pearls!

They are much too precious to waste
And toss out in the trash
In each one is a million smiles
A million giggles, grins and laughs!

So I took your little tooth
While you slept last night
But left you a little present
I hope that was all right!

?

I hope you didn't mind
But you were sleeping
When I came in your room tonight
So I didn't turn on the light.

But I took your little tooth with me
(Such a beautiful tooth to see)
And left you a gift instead
Under the pillow neath your head.

211

I Would Not Change A Thing About You

From the first time that I saw you
And you were handed into my waiting arms
I was awed by how perfect you were
So sweet with babyish charms.

The years have come and gone
Oh so swiftly have they flown
And these years I've been your mom
Are the happiest I've know.

I treasure every moment
I love the things you say and do
And still I find in this heart of mine
I would not change a thing about you!

Happy Valentines Day to my daughter
My joy and treasure you will always be
And I am forever thankful
That God sent you to me.

?

When I grow up
And choose what I want to do
I want to be a mommy
Exactly like you!

In My Heart's Eyes

In the eyes of my heart
This is how I will always see you
This is how you will always be
Smiling, cuddly and tiny
So sweetly looking up at me.

If I should live to be 100
Or if older than that I shall be
This is the picture in my heart's eyes
That I shall take to Heaven with me.

?

Little Bird

Like a tiny baby bird
Your sweet lips are open wide
As I bend to kiss you
I see the smile inside.

Like a little baby lamb
So bundled up and cozy
As I touch your little face
I see your cheeks so rosy.

Like any tiny baby cub
That wants to play so sweetly
As my heart joins with yours
I love you so completely!

"How Much Do You Love Me, Mommy?

"How much do you love me, Mommy?"
I heard my darling say
And then with her teddy bear
She ran outside to play...

How much I thought?
Oh you cannot begin to know
Even if I tried
To tell you so!

You know the joy
Of finding caterpillars in the Spring
And the happiness that
A new toy can bring...

You know how much fun
It is to go play
With a brand new friend
And stay all day...

Do you remember on Christmas
How you exclaimed in delight
At all of the packages
So colorful and bright...

Think back to the fireworks
On the fourth of July
(I remember the joy
That I saw in your eyes!)

Think of all the wonderful
Things that you know
How you love the sunshine in summer
And in the winter the snow...

And then my little one
Come and ask me again
And mommy will have a place
When she can begin...

A Thousand Words

They say a picture is worth 1000 words
But this one is worth more
It says so many sweet
and wonderful things
That in my heart I'll store.

How could I begin to tell
Of the sweetness of your cherub face
Or describe your sweet smelling baby skin
And the softness of your embrace?

How I explain the light in your eyes
When you smiled at me
I need more than 1000 words
Because you are so precious to me.

This picture is such a treasure
It reminds of this special day
I keep it close to remind me of the joy that is you
When I run out of words to say.

They say a picture is worth 1000 words
But this one is worth more...

The Almost Missed Day

"Come on Mommy and let's have fun!"
Words from my daughter and from my son.
"Oh sweethearts, Mommy has so much to do
I'm so sorry that I can't play with you."

"Come out Daddy, come on outside
You look for me and I'll go hide!"
"Sorry, little one but I have to go
But I wish I could, I hope you know!"

Then I felt a tugging at my heart
Right in the tender "mommy" part
And in that instant my heart knew
Exactly what I had to do...

Looking down at wistful faces
Was that my voice that I heard say
"Come on sweet baby, and let's go play
Housework can wait for some other day!"

"Join us Daddy and come home early today
For this whole family is going to play!
Round up your brother and sister and all our pets
For this day will be our most fun yet!"

Work will be there when we get done
But my family and I are going to have some fun!
And years from now we will remember this
That this was the day we ALMOST missed!

Work will be there when we get done
But my family and I are going
to have some fun!

Another Name for Sunshine

Written for MB member

Kendall is another name for sunshine
She brings sunshine to our world
She loves colors bright and sunny
She's mommy's sunshine girl!

Kendall finds delight
In everything she does
And in her room are all the things
That our Kendall loves.

The sun above shines down
On this sweet little girl
As the glow from her sweet face
Brightens up our world!

Baby's Kissing Spot

Angels bending down to earth
Kissed my darling from her birth
Until on her tiny head she's got
A tiny little kissing spot!

The hair was sweetly worn away
From being kissed day after day.
How precious is that spot to me
A reminder of love that I can see!

And every day since she's been born
I kiss her on that spot so worn
And I thank the Heavenly Father above
For this darling He sent for me to love!

Baby Doll

I have a special friend
Who is with me all the time
She wears a tiny satin gown
This baby doll of mine.

She goes where I want to go
And I love her very much
She brings comfort to me every night
For she stays close enough for me to touch.

We snuggle up together
And to make sure that she feels safe
I keep her close beside me
Wrapped up in my embrace.

And in the morning when I awake
She has stayed right by my side
Ready to get up and face the day
To go shopping or for a ride.

She might awake before me
But if she does, she doesn't stir
For she likes to always be with me
And I take her everywhere!

I have a special friend
Who is with me all the time
She wears a tiny satin gown
This baby doll of mine.

Perfect Child

My brother got a spanking
Mommy tanned his little hide
For he took away my bike
And wouldn't let me ride.

Mommy didn't see him
But I saw him pick a flower
From the neighbor's garden
Within the very hour.

I thought that I should tell her
'Cause she really needs to know
In case the neighbors wonder
Why their garden doesn't grow.

Sister got a scolding
'Cause she was very bad
She took away my candy bar
And it was the only one I had.

Daddy didn't know it
So I told him what I knew
That sister told a lie today
And said that it was true!

I try to help my parents out
And be a model kid
If it were not for me
They wouldn't know what the others did!

I was very good today
And not a bit of trouble
When the other kids were wild
Oh what stress it is
To be a perfect child!

Lovely in Lace

My heart is in my throat
As I look at you
So sweet and lovely in lace
With such a sweet expression on your face.

This moment will stay in my mind
And the memory will remain in my heart
And will cheer me in those times
When we may be far apart.

And each time I kiss your cheek
And feel your sweet embrace
I will remember how precious you are
And how absolutely lovely in lace!

?

It's ME!
Yesterday I went to bed
And I was only FIVE.
But today when I awoke
SIX years I've been alive!

Just in case you don't recognize
The older girl you see
I thought that I should tell you
IT'S ME! IT'S ME! IT'S ME!!
(or Mommy says "It is I!")

My Dear Stepdaughter

My Dear Stepdaughter,
You may not know this
And you may not think you care.
But I've something on my heart
That I really want to share.

I've never tried to take the place
Of the mother who gave you life,
But I have grown to love you more and more
In the years that I've been your father's wife.

It's more than just the "stepmother" deal--
It's very genuine the love I feel.
I mean every act of love I do
To show you how I feel about you.

If I knew that I could make a wish
And be assured that it would come true
I would ask for our family to be happy together
And that we could spend more time with you.

I'm making this album for you and
I've loved doing each little part.
I hope that you will find in it's pages
Something that will touch your heart.

I hope that you will keep it forever
And treasure the love inside.
Remembering the love and laughter
As well as the tears we've cried.

And know that even though I'm a stepmother
And some tough times you have been through
The love that I feel is valid and real
And I will always love you.

221

NATURE

God has created a beautiful world for us and it is up to us to use it and not abuse it. It is up to us to see the beauty in every aspect of His handiwork and consider it with awe and respect.

God has created such delicate, beautiful, artistic, colorful and even humorous creatures on land and sea that our imaginations could not even begin to compare with what He has designed and created.

From the delicate fragile wings of a butterfly to the enormous whale... each creature is a work of art by the Master Artist!

Within this chapter you will find poems from the tiny ant to the lovely zebra for your enjoyment.

?

God doesn't color
Within the lines
His colors aren't subdued
His artwork on earth and sky
Is the loveliest to be viewed.

About His Art Work

God's Sunset

I look around me at the beauty
Unequaled on this early sod
A masterpiece of color
Painted by the Hand of God.

What lovely colors in His palette
And what tones and hues are infused.
All the wonders at His disposal
Did our Heavenly Father use.

I will never take for granted
The beauty that I see
For it is sent to us from Heaven
As a gift for you and me.

God's Colors

Let the beauty
Which God bestows
On this earthly realm
Remind you that
On this ship called life,
God is at the helm!

God doesn't color
Within the lines
His colors aren't subdued
His artwork on earth and sky
Is the loveliest to be viewed.

God's Paint Box

I stand in awe
Of the colors above me
A sky fashioned by the hand
Of a God who loves me.

Colors so vibrant
So pure and so true
A sky painting that only
Our God could do.

No earthly artist
Could conceive in
Paint or mind
Such color and majesty
Of the Divine!

I Love Your Colors!

I love your colors, Lord!
I love the way you paint the world
And every day I see even more
Of your artistry unfurled.

Each time I see a leafy tree
Or blossoms of pink or white
My heart rejoices at the scene
And I marvel at the sight!

Colors so vibrant
So pure and so true...

God's Rainbow—His Promise

When I see a rainbow
In the Heavens up above
I'm reminded of God's promise
And in awe of God's Great Love!

When I see the colors
So beautiful and bright
I am reminded of how God above
Brought the earth to light.

The rainbow reminds me
Of the promise God gave you and me
And that He sends us a promise
That we all look up and see!

?

The Promise

The Rainbow is a promise
Signed up in the sky
By a God that loves His children
Enough to send a sign
That His Word is always true
And His will Devine.

I love to see the rainbow
After the rain falls down
For it is like a special love letter
With a message so profound!

The Waterfall

Beauty surrounds us
In one form or another
In our families and friends
And our love for each other.

God gave us such wonderful
Sights to behold
More beautiful than can be bought
With silver or gold.

And among my favorites
This sight above all
Is majestic and stirring
A grand waterfall!

A Thank You Poem to God

Thank you Lord for the beautiful things
That you through your gift of Nature bring.

Thank you for each deer or doe
And lovely woods where they may go.

Thank for the beautiful rivers and streams
And lovely little animal beings!

Thank you for each flower and tree
And for two eyes that I might see!

Thank you for the air we breathe
And for all of Your blessings we receive!
Amen

Master Artist

The teacher glanced at the offering
That a little child had brought...
A picture of the sky—
It was approval that she sought.

"How lovely," the teacher said,
And touched the sweet ones cheek
But in truth she thought the talent
Of this one was really weak!

The sky wasn't sky blue at all,
And there were no distinguishing lines
There were wild and vivid pinks and blues...
And nothing well defined...

She praised the child for what she had done
And in her heart she thought
That this one would do much better
Once she had been taught.

And then one day the teacher rose
And got an early start
And looking toward the sky...
SHE SAW THE LITTLE CHILD'S ART!

The teacher glanced at the offering
That a little child had brought...

Embrace Life

Always embrace Life
Whatever your age
With heart full of love
And arms opened wide.

Embrace life as a child
And then as you mature
For each day is special
And nothing's for sure.

So treasure each moment
For what life might bring
Hug Winter time close
And dance in the Spring!

Sunshine and Rain

People love sunshine
But fear the pain
That they feel in their hearts
Comes with the rain.
Sunshine brings lightness
To soul and heart
And storm clouds remind us
Of things torn apart.

But how would we know
How good it could be
To dance in the sunlight
If no storms we could see.
In both I have found joy
In both I have had pain
I have cried in the sunshine
And I have danced in the rain.

About His Animals and Insects, etc...

You Can't Hug A Frog...

Some people like all kinds of pets
From dogs and cats to mice
But as for the perfect pet for me...
I think frogs are nice!

Frogs are very easy to please
And like to live in a stream
Frogs are always very nice--
I've never seen a frog that's mean!

People hug their cats and
They cuddle with their dogs
Now you can hold one in your hand
But you can't hug a frog!

Nope! You really cannot hug a frog
And this is not a joke...
You can't hug a frog
Or it might
croak...

You Can't Hug a Frog Or It Might Croak...

The Dragonfly

Nothing save the human eye
Can record the beauty
Of the dragonfly
No film can capture
And hold forever
It's jewel like colors
No, not ever!

Like the most glittering of jewels
On wispy wings they flit around
As our hearts with joy abound
Oh, light little dragonfly, on the ground!

People all around the world
Seem enamored
With tiny bit of fragile entomology
And proclaim it a lovely sight to see.

I love you little dragonfly
Insect seems too tame a name
For a creature so lovely to view
For I see such delicate artwork
Used by Our Creator in you!

?

Like the most glittering of jewels
On wispy wings they flit around...
As our hearts with joy abound
Oh, light little dragonfly, on the ground!

Plethora of Dragonflies

What joy and happiness
Could befall me
Did my ears hear the
Dragonflies call me?

There on the path
In front of me
A plethora of dragonflies
Did I see.

They were all tiny and dainty
With fragile silky wing
And did my ears deceive me or
Did I hear a dragonfly sing?

But as I watching them
Flitting to and fro
In such a lovely place
I felt a plethora of dragonflies
Give me a dragonfly embrace!

?

There on the path
In front of me
A plethora of dragonflies
Did I see.

Fleeting Dragonfly

As fleeting as the dragonfly
Whose filmy wings forever beat
To keep it air loft in the wind
So is the rush of children's feet.

Celebrating the warmth of sunny days
And yearning all Winter long for Spring
They laugh and yell and giggle
At the first sign of balmy breeze.

Opening wide Winter's closed doors
Which were battened down right after Fall
A child always knows that Spring is coming soon
And is the best season of them all.

So celebrate with us the signs of Spring
And watch for the little dragonfly to come
Reminding us how fleeting are childhood days
And to treasure memories... each and every one!

?

As fleeting as the dragonfly
Whose filmy wings forever beat
To keep it air loft in the wind
So is the rush of children's feet.

The Butterfly

Like the creature we know
Whose life progresses in different stages
Until it becomes the beautiful butterfly
So am I progressing.

Let me not stay too long
In the caterpillar stage
Spending my life eating and growing
Without even knowing all I can be.

But let my appetite
Be only for your Word
And things from you.
Let my growth be steady and sure
And let me mature in You.

After I'm no longer a babe
Let me enter the pupa stage needing a teacher
As a pupa needs something solid to hold onto
Using this time to grow in You.

Then Dear Lord, let me burst forth
As an adult, ready to fly
Carrying pollen from flower to flower
Helping others to grow
Spreading what I know
Reflecting the beauty of Your love
In the sunshine
As your butterfly.

Then Dear Lord,
Let me burst forth...

Wooly Little Pillar

Wooly Little Caterpillar
Where are you going?
I see you in the sunshine
But never when it's snowing!

I think you are so beautiful
And I think it's really neat
That you have lots of tiny legs
But you have no feet!!

ANTS

I went on a picnic
And didn't tell a soul
I wanted to be alone
And in complete control!

I spread my blanket on the ground
Right next to beautiful shady plants
And what do you think I saw--
A tiny little group of ants!

How do they always know
Where I shall picnic
Or when I am going to eat?
Do they have a built in satellite
That tracks my own two feet!

And if they are so industrious
This point I'd like to share
How come when I have a party
The ants are always there!!

This BUGS Me!

I've ants in my plants
And slugs on my sidewalk
And beetles in my begonia again.
I've snails on the zinnias
And bugs that meanie ones
It seems that I just can't win!

I've no solution to be rid of them
And there are things I prefer instead of them
But I don't think I shall ever be
Really alone in my little country home
Totally and completely bug free!

So, I have made my resolution
That my only solution
May be to just plant more than I need
And try to inspire those who travel so far
To munch their lunch on a weed.

Pretty Little Lady (Bug)

Pretty little lady
Dressed in your Sunday best
All dolled up in red
With black dots upon your vest!
I hold you on my hand
Wish I could give a hug
To my dainty little friend
A little ladybug!

Have You Ever Fought a Rooster?

Now you can fight a chicken
They are might poor at pickin'
Out a really good place to start a fight.

You can fight a "banty hen"
'Cause when all their tiny peckin' begins
All you have to do is step away.

But whatever else you do sir
Don't try to fight a rooster
'Cause you will be the looser in the end.

They will peck you and they will spur you
'Til Lloyds of London won't insure ya
So don't ever fight a rooster
My dear friends.

You can fight a little 'possum
Or a mad dog or a bull
And you might have a good chance to get away.
But if you see a mean ole rooster
Coming at ya and determined
Better just get down on your knees and pray!

?

All of God's creatures
Big and small,
All of God's creatures
He made them all.
Written by CC Milam

A Day At the Zoo

What could be as much fun
As a day at the zoo?
Watching to see
What the monkeys will do?

What fun to watch
A giraffe so tall
Or to see a Panda
Curled up in a ball!

I love to see
Lions and tigers (Oh, my!)
And the snakes are so scary
But I didn't cry!

I loved the birds
High up in the trees
And the Penguins so cold
That I thought they would freeze!

But my favorite thing
About the trip to the zoo
Was all of the fun I had
Being there with you!

?

What could be as much fun
As a day at the zoo?

You Belong in the Zoo!

Look at you
You are as tall as can be
So much taller than
Daddy and me!

Your neck is long
Your ears are pointed
And look at those legs...
Are they double jointed?

I love the color of your hide
I like the way your spots are wide
You are such fun to see
You are just like a giraffe should be!

The Giraffe

Nature has many wonderful sights
Lovely to behold
None are lovelier to my eyes
Than giraffes of brown and gold.

Tall and lean they stand
On legs much taller than my head
They would lose their mystery
If they stood on stubby legs instead!

So enjoy your bears and chipmunks
And cuddle those koala bears
But when I go to the zoo or park
The giraffe my deep affection shares!

The Zebra

I would love to have a zebra
To ride to school each day
For people would be so surprised
They would give me the right of way!

No longer would I stand in line
Or being in a traffic jam
For I would ride right on past
On my zebra I'd call Sam!

The Panda

I love to watch the Panda Bear
Playing at the zoo.
I could stare at them all day
To see what they would do.

The beauty of the Panda
Is almost beyond compare
God created a masterpiece
In the Panda Bear!

?

God created a Masterpiece
In the Panda Bear!

Alligator

Pity the poor crocodile
Who really never learned to smile
And has to wear a scaly skin
And is only loved by next of kin!

And the alligator
Is not any better
His skin is rough
In all kinds of weather!

I think they would like to be
Safe and dry like you and me
But maybe they don't mind a bit
And soft unwrinkled skin would never fit!

The Kangaroo

The kangaroo is a funny sight
With her legs on loose
And her ears on tight...
With great big feet on the bottom
And tiny legs on top,
It's a wonder that a Roo can hop!
A kangaroo is strange to see
With a pouch in front
To hold her new baby...
Although a roo looks funny to some
I guess she is beautiful to another one
And when she looks at me (or you)
She probably prefers the look of a kangaroo!

About His Seasons

My Favorite Season of All

If I had to decide on
My favorite season of all
I wouldn't say summer
I would say Fall.

I love the crispness in the air
And the colors so bold and bright
And the way the trees look
In the early morning's light.

I love the gentle ways
The leaves waft to the ground
They dance daintily and silently
Until they seem to surround...

I know that Winter is not far behind
But that does not bother me
As I happily play in the colorful leaves
That are piled up to my knees.

?

If I had to decide on
My favorite season of all...

Autumn

God dipped His hand into the sun
And spread its gold upon the trees
Like gleaming torches touched with flame
They leap and dance in Fall's brisk breeze.

A chill wind twirls fingers through the leaves
And they give up their fragile hold
A drifting curtain sifting down to
Crimson carpet bright and bold.

High overhead a skein of geese
Knits patterns there for all to see
The leader calls out to the flock
Haunting,
Honking,
Harmony.

Written by my lovely friend
Ural Donohoe and used by permission

Fall

Listen carefully and you can hear
The gentle whisper of leaves
Falling ever so softly
To the
Ground.
I can hear the silence
I can feel the calm
But most of all,
I love the quietness
of
Fall.

I Love Fall!

I love the seasons!
I love them all
But my favorite season
Has to be FALL!

I love the trees so bright
With colors of orange and brown
And how very pretty the leaves
Look when scattered on the ground!

I love to rake them all in a pile
And then jump around in them for a while.
Then I lay down on the ground
And gather the leaves all around.

Could any thing be more fun than to play
In the beautiful colorful leaves all day?
That is why my favorite season of all
Should be, could be, HAS TO BE FALL!!

?

I Love the Seasons!
I Love Them All
But My Favorite Season
Has to Be FALL!

Fall In Love in Autumn

Autumn comes so gently
With natures paintbrush in its hands
It only whispers gentle things
And never makes demands.

First a little streak of red
A little streak of gold
And then the brown takes over
By the time the weather's cold.

I fell in love in the autumn time
As nature perfected its lovely art
You came so sweetly into my life
And stole away my heart.

I knew in the Autumn I loved you
And knew that the whole year through
I would look back with fondness
On the day I knew I loved you.

Look at What I've Found

Look at what I've found
A fall tree looks like an arm (of brown)
Connected to a hand like mine
With fingers as the branches bold
That the colorful leaves of fall can hold.

I Fell in Love in
the Autumn Time...

244

Fall Aboard!

Summer is done
and
Winter is on the way.
But that's no reason
To sit and fret...
We still have time
To play!

Fall aboard!
And let's jump
In the leaves
And skate on the
Sidewalks until
Fall disappears
And winter appears
And the sound of
Our skates is stilled!

?

Fall aboard!
And let's jump
In the leaves!

Winter's Whispers

If you listen
You can hear it
Whispers soft and low.
It means that winter is coming
With delicate flakes of snow.

If you stop for a moment
And take a look around
You can hear winter's whisper
And it is a lovely sound.

The first snowflakes fall softly
And cover up the earth
Providing nature's winter cover
So Spring can bring new birth.

Listen to the whisper
And enjoy winter's grace
Look up toward Heaven
And let the flakes fall on your face.

?

Come outside
In the snow and play
And let's make angels
For fun today!

Lay down in the snow
And flap your wings
And we will look like
Angel beings!

Snowman Soup

Good friends good fun good treats
In sunny or snowy weather
Share a bit of chocolate
And celebrate being together.

Candy canes and kisses
Are good for anytime
And I'm so happy to share them
With special friends of mine!

So mix a bit of chocolate drink
And pop in a marshmallow or two
And soon your snowman soup
Will make you feel warmer through and through!

Snow Angels

Little Angel in the snow
Looks just like someone we know...
Oh my goodness! Now I see
The little snow angel is ME!

?

Good friends good fun good treats
In sunny or snowy weather
Share a bit of chocolate
And celebrate being together.

Snow Friend Like You

What fun it is to build
A friend with which to play.
He will stand close by your side
And never move away!

What fun to decide on
What he will wear
On the shape of his nose
And the kind of hair!

You can make him tall
And make him thin
You can undo his figure
And start over again!

You can dress him in a dapper way
Or like a kid going out to play!
You can give him a scarf and hat
Or a baseball mitt and a wooden bat!

But just one thing
You must know
Your friend will melt
In the sun's warm glow!

Spring

Thank you Lord
For beautiful Spring
It is so special to me
Watching the earth
Come back in rebirth
Reminds me of your gift to me!

248

Snow

People in the tropics
Will never know
The fun and excitement
Of playing in the snow!

I love the feel of new fallen snow
Drifting by my face.
I love the look of soft white flakes
Like dainty bits of lace.

I love waking in the morning
To see snow all around
Covering up the streets
And every patch of ground!

I love the thrill of walking
With those I love
Hand in hand in hand
And glove in glove in glove!

I love to wear brand new boots
Cause last years just won't fit
Oh how I love the snow
Every part of it!!

I love the look of soft white flakes
Like dainty bits of lace...

Waiting for Summer

I know how happy you are my dear
That summer and sunshine are finally here!
I love the way you love each day
And all the funny games you play!

I love the look on your sticky little face
When a melting Popsicle you embrace,
And the way you play outside with your friends
You would love to play till daylight ends!

You don't like it when I say come inside
But I know that you need your rest
And sometimes even in the summertime
A mommy knows what's best!

I love the summer and I love you
For once I was a summer kid too,
And caught fireflies in a glass
And played hide and seek in the grass.

Oh yes, how sweet it was to be free
You bring out the love of summer in me
And everything you say and do
Just keeps on reminding me why I love you!!!

Summer Sounds

I love the sounds of summer
I love it more each day
For summertime means the sun is out
And warms me as I play!

Lazy Hazy Summer Day

Lazy, hazy summer day
Come and take my cares away
I'm tired of work
And want to play!
Summer breezes and summer fun
Summer clothes and summer shoes
Farewell blahs and winter blues!
Summer, hurry and come to stay...
Oh how I love a summer day
Lazy, hazy summer day!

Sun Kisses

Today I played out in the summer sun
And it felt so nice and cozy
I felt as if kissed by its rays
On face and arms and nosey.

Today I ran and played and laughed
Out in the summer sun
It was such a lovely day
And I was having so much fun!

But when I came inside the house
From my day of playing in the yard
My nose and cheeks and legs...
Had been kissed a bit too hard!

My face was nice and bright
My nose was awfully pink
Next time I play out in the sun
I'll wear a hat I think!!

I Love Summer

I Love Summer!
I love it most of all!
You can keep your Winter snow
And Autumn leaves that fall!

I love the sounds of Summer
I love it more each day,
I love the sounds of Summer kids
As they romp and run and play.

I love the sounds that crickets make
And I love to hear the little frog
With his deep throaty song
As he sits and croaks upon a log.

I love the sounds of birds that fly
And love the songs they sing
I love the smell of Summer grass
And watching children swing!

I love the sounds of cars driving past
On pavement heated by the sun
For I know a good warm day
Equals lots of Summer fun!

I love the sounds of Summer
I love the look and feel of it
I love the green and velvet grass
Oh, I just love it every bit!

I Love Summer!

About His Flowers and Plants

Apple Picking

We went apple picking
And we had so much fun
We had fewer in our bags than in our tummy
Before our apple picking day was done.

The trees were so beautiful
With apples on each limb
We jumped as high as we could
And tried to reach more of them.

I loved our apple-picking day
And our apples were so delicious
We had a yummy fun filled day
That was also quite nutritious.

Perfect Food

Apples are the perfect food
At least that's what they say,
To eat an apple every day
The doctors keeps away!

I don't know about the doctor
Or if what they say is true.
I just know I love my apples
But I will gladly share with you!

I love to go and pick them
off the big ole leafy tree.
Apple trees are so much fun to climb
And beautiful to see!

253

Nature's Picker Upper, Watermelon

You cannot be a grumpy gus
Or a sour puss for long
For once you bite into a juicy slice of melon
Your heart may burst into song!

Tree Climber

I love those warm summer days
So that I can go outside and play
Enjoying the sun and a summer breeze
While laying in the grass or climbing trees!

I love to stand on tippy toe
And stretch as far as I can
So that the lowest branch
Is finally within my hand!

I love to pull myself up
Climbing limb to limb so high
Until I feel like part of the tree
Framed against the sky!

I feel like a bird as I look around
Closer to the sky than to the ground!
I think a bird must really be blessed
To live in a tree in a warm little nest!

I Love those Warm Summer Days...

Why Do Willows Weep?

Why do willows weep?
I do not know
Perhaps their tears
Help them to grow.

I only know that
When I walk with you there
I have only smiles
And happiness to share.

Sunflowers

Sunflowers stand tall
With leafy arms outstretched all day
Providing shelter from the sun
To little kids at play.

No one would wear them on wrist corsage
Or place them in a lapel
But standing outside
In God's fields all day
What a lovely story
They have to tell!

Sunflower you are giant
Among the flowers
A spectacular sight to behold
One of nature's beauties
And Dakota's Gold!

Bluebonnet Time

Texas in the Springtime
Is such a lovely sight
Feast your eyes upon the landscape
And you find there pure delight!

Little ladylike flowers in their bonnets
Colored such a lovely hue
There is no film nor camera can preserve it
Such a luscious shade of blue.

Texas must look a lot like Heaven
When the Bluebonnets bloom in the Spring
And cover the roadsides in their carpets
Filling the state the delight they bring!

Bluebonnets

Loved since man first trod the Texas prairies
Surrounded by fascinating folk lore
Bluebonnets have not faded in their beauty
But have grown beautiful all the more...

Myths surround them and the telling
Grows into ballads that we sing
Applauding all of the beauty
That the simple Bluebonnet brings!

Texas in the Springtime
Is such a lovely sight...

Where Did You Come From?

Where did you come from little flower?
Where did you get your lovely name?
Is it because you look like lovely ladies
Playing hide and seek...in nature's game?

Did you come over with the Spanish?
Or did you welcome them when they arrived?
For centuries you have grown wild here
And we are most blessed that you survived.

Springtime would not be the same without you
And kids would not gasp in sheer delight
When they experience a Texas Springtime
And their young eyes upon you light.

Poinsettia Passion

You don't see them in the
Summer or the Spring!
But when winter comes
And snowflakes fall
And Christmas is around the bend
Poinsettias pop up everywhere
With each one having a twin!
You see them in the market.
You see them in the shops.
They are displayed everywhere
In big ceramic pots!
It makes my mom so happy
When poinsettias are the fashion
Because her heart is filled
With such poinsettia passion!!

Freedom Blooms

We bask in freedom's lovely light
And enjoy the blooms nature has in store.
Flowers kissed by Heaven's sun
Are evident shore to shore.

Even the rocks that God provides
Seem content for all to see
That we love our country
Shore to shore
And sea to shinning sea!

Look at the Flowers

Look at the flowers
As you drive by
See how the colors
Look so bright against the sky?

Look at the flowers
As you go about your day
Of making life more fun
Flowers have a way!

A Weed?

The thistle is a weed they say
And no respect does it obtain
But those that some would deem a weed
I call by another name.

A weed clutched in the fist
Of a tiny lass or lad
Has more power to cheer the heart
Than any expensive orchid
Will have or ever had.

Won't You Come Into My Garden?

Won't you come into my garden
My little one so dear?
The flowers have a little song
I'd love for you to hear...

Listen for their music
In the quietness of the day
Their leaves rustle in the breeze
In a sweet melodic way.

I ask this little favor little one
If this one thing you would do
Won't you come into my garden?
I'd love my flowers to see you...

Loving the Lake

It is so refreshing
When a boat ride
We can take
To commune with nature
And just love and enjoy the lake.

We love the peace and quiet
The water is still and serene
And the beauty of the surroundings
Rivals anything we've seen.

It is so nice to take time out
For a sweet refreshing break
Spend quality time with each other
And go boating on the lake.

Sunshine and Rain

People love sunshine
But fear the pain
That they feel in their hearts
Comes with the rain.

Sunshine brings lightness
To soul and heart
And storm clouds remind us
Of things torn apart.

But how would we know
How good it could be
To dance in the sunlight
If no storms we could see.

In both I have found joy
In both I have had pain
I have cried In the sunshine
And I have danced in the rain.

In both I have found joy
In both I have had pain
I have cried In the sunshine
And I have danced in the rain.

And After the California Fire

Bless Our State

I will no longer take for granted, Lord
No matter how long it lasts
The fragrance of a blooming flower
Or a single blade of grass.

For I got a glimpse today Lord
Of a world without flower or tree
And it broke my heart ere I saw
Just how barren our world would be.

I will treasure each of your creations
Be they on hoof or wing
And will bless each sweet melody
That your breezes play in the spring.

And I would ask you now, Lord
As I humbly bow my knee
That you bless my state
Each blade of grass
And each and every tree!

Amen

PATRIOTIC

Why We Are Still Crying
Written after the Columbia tragedy

As with every major event of devastation and disaster, terrorism and space tragedy, certain questions eventually arise. Some people have asked why these lives are more important than those lost in any other way? Why are we as a nation or even as a world continually mourning this loss? Why is there so much media attention? Why the songs, the poems, the news coverage day after day?

Aside from the whole space program, the importance of the program, the marvels that we have witnessed and learned, the shock of the loss and the magnitude and awful trauma of it. I believe there is more.

Most of us, if not all of us have lost loved ones. Some of us have lost them by tragic means and others by illness, accidents or old age. We mourn those we've lost and then are encouraged to get over it and get on with life. That is good in theory, but in truth, the hurt and sense of loss never entirely goes away and never will.

When we have a national emergency, a national loss of the magnitude of Sept 11, the Challenger or the Columbia, we are drawn together as a family, a city, a nation and even a world family that can grieve together. It reminds us of the sanctity and fragility of human life and lets us grieve not only for the nation's loss but also for our own.

We comfort each other for the loss of our heroes and in giving and receiving that comfort it serves us in our past grief as well.

If we were to continually mourn and mention the loss of our parents or grandparents, etc day after day, soon the world would tire of listening to us, but when we share the pain and sorrow of these high profile events, it becomes ok to mourn and let your tears flow freely.

So, I will mourn for the loss of the space heroes, I assign them no heroic place in Heaven, no guardianship of my journeys or flights any more so than that belonging to my parents or grandparents. I don't see them as stars in the sky or angels protecting me. I am too much of a Bible scholar to ascribe anything that exceptional to them. I leave that to my Creator, but I do see them as 7 souls who are now in eternity and I weep for those families left behind and I appreciate the sacrifice these heroes have made.

Yes, they are heroes. I take nothing away from them. But also to me, those that I have loved and lost are heroes too. They had no medals or honors and got no news coverage but were and are every bit as dear to me as these wonderful men and women are to their families. And as I have shed tears while learning more and more about them as individuals, I also shed tears for parents, grandparents, dear friends and family who have also joined in eternity's ranks.

So, let us weep for these fine men and women and for those dear to us. Know that we realize that those you love are missed just as deeply and for just as long. In this section are poems regarding this tragedy as well as the horrible events of September 11th along with other patriotic verses.

NEVER FORGET

Never forget that in a moment
The course of history can change.
Events of such magnitude can happen
That the world will never be the same.

We will never forget the men and women
Who stand with courage, valor and pride,
Ready to protect against all manner of foe,
Nor will we forget the ones who've died.

With heartfelt appreciation we see the Firemen
Waiting for the signal that their skill is needed.
Thankfully we remember battles they so valiantly fought
Worn and weary until they had succeeded.

In deepest gratitude we see the Policemen.
Always vigilant they must stay
Ready to protect and serve
Cognizant that danger lurks in each ordinary day.

We will not forget the EMT's
Nor as heroes count them less.
They respond with utmost efficiency
And pass the cruelest tests.

We must never forget the heroes
Created on that awful September day
When those who wished us harm
So maliciously took so many lives away.

American heroes live everywhere
And in all shapes and sizes come,
Armed with a love of God and country
Rather than a gun.

A gun alone cannot protect
It is only good in part.
The fierce desire to defend our nation
Begins deep within the human heart.

Let us vow to remember always
And treat as the national treasures that they are,
Those who protect us against our enemies
Be they evil men, famine, flood, or fire.

Written for and appeared in
Never Forget Campaign by PCCrafter

So Close to Home

So close to home, Lord
They were so close to home today
When the Columbia broke apart
And took seven souls away.

So close to home, Lord
And to the ones they love
But now they are home with You Lord
In Your Heaven up above.

So close to home, yes
Close to the ones who waited so happily
But instead they went to Your house
To start their eternity.
In Remembrance of February 1, 2003

Let Us Vow to Remember ALWAYS

Can't Stop Crying

I can't stop crying Lord
Can you make the pain go away?
Another tragedy has hit
On our precious earth today!

We watched in awe and wonder
As the shuttle hit the skies above
And planned to welcome heroes home
With hearts full of pride and love

But today the worst has happened
And 7 souls were lost to flame
As the Columbia was shattered
When it hit the earth again.

There are now 7 new souls in Heaven
And that each is precious to you we know
But, Lord there are weeping families here
In whose hearts there is now a hole.

Please wrap your arms around those weeping
And give them your loving care
And remind each child of yours on earth
To remember them in prayer.

My eyes are filled with tears
And my heart is filled with pain
But I know that when eternity comes
We will all be reunited again.
In Remembrance of February 1, 2003

Remember them in prayer...

Heroes

When we remember our nation's heroes
From that cruel September day,
Let us realize that men of valor
Do not instantly become that way.

A hero is not created in an instant—
One deed and then it's done.
A hero's compassion is instilled at birth
His deed shows us that he's one.

There are heroes in training all about us
In sizes large and small.
Some who are but infants now
Will someday answer a hero's call.
The ones who serve daily as fireman
As policeman and EMT's
As circumstance and duty calls them out
Heroes they soon could be.

Consider the military men and women too
Who daily risk their lives for you.
Theirs is such a daunting task
But never for accolades do they ask.

Look at your fellow passengers on a train
Or those who travel with you by air
Look at the seats around you
A hero may be sitting there.

A hero is built within in the heart
And let us not forget
They live with us and surround us...
We just don't know it yet!
In Remembrance of September 11, 2001

267

For Our Neighbors

Forgive us dear friends and neighbors
In countries around the world
Forgive us when our eyes tear up
When we see our flag unfurled.

For we are a very patriotic country
Though sometimes we make mistakes
But when one American is lost
It causes each American heart to break.

And when we see your love outpoured
As you witness and feel our pain
Our hearts are filled with love for you
That in our souls forever will remain.

In humble gratitude we thank you
For sharing our joys and sorrows
And we pray that for our whole wide world
There will be a more joyous tomorrow.

?

What Does A Hero Look Like?

What does a hero look like?
It's really hard to say.
A hero looks like the EMT
Who goes to work each day.

A hero looks like a neighbor
Who is easily within your view.
A hero looks like a policeman
And a hero looks like YOU!

We Will Never Forget

You are our heroes and we honor you
Those of you who died and those who survived.
Even though we may not know your names
Each brother, sister, husband and wife.

Heroes of all shapes and sizes
Fought the flames and lead others to safety.
Heroes comforted the sick and dying
And dried the tears of those who were crying.

Firefighters, policemen and EMT's
All those whose daily work placed them in danger
We will never forget what you did that day
Intent on helping others, you went out of your way.

You went to work when it was your day off.
You heard duty call and you responded
In the only way a hero could reply
You grabbed your gear and said, "Here am I."

So many heroes were born that day
And in the same day so many died.
So many hearts were broken that day
And so many tears were cried.

We will never forget you and all you did for us
We will forever keep your memory alive
For because of you, we have today.
Because of you our nation will survive.
In Remembrance of September 11, 2001

Because of You Our Nation Will Survive...

269

God Bless Our American Heroes

These people who traveled to Heaven by plane
Have not bled and died in vain.
Forever now our nations refrain—
God Bless these American Heroes!

Who would think a child of four
A baby still and hardly more
Would join in the heroes ranks
With never a chance for childish pranks!

Her life cut off in a hateful way
As she flew home that fateful day
Never again to run and play!
God Bless this American Hero!

Business men and women too
We all wonder if they knew
That their fate was sealed
What plans had those fanatics revealed.
God Bless these American Heroes!

As fireman prepared to start their day
Kissed their families and sped away
Knowing not what lay ahead
Some would perish, would soon be dead
God Bless these American Heroes!

And still at home some sit and wait
On their calendars marking that date
When life and happiness seemed to end
Waiting for news that someone will send
God Bless these American Heroes!

And people from both far and near
Send prayers, love and words of cheer
Telling families that they care
That in this grief we all must share
God Bless these American Heroes!

And God Bless you
And God Bless me
And let our nation always be
Worthy of our American Heroes!
In Remembrance of September 11, 2001

God Bless

God bless those folks
Who every day
Take the time
To kneel and pray
For those who daily
Risk their life
In wartime turmoil
Conflicts and strife.

God bless those folks
Who wait at home
For those they love
And call their own
And who have shed
so many tears
While trying to overcome their fears.
God bless those folks.

God Bless You!

And the World Mourns

We forget sometimes that the entire world
Is connected as if by a thread.
And every time a tragedy hits
It is as if the whole world has bled.

We forget sometimes how precious is life
And how fragile a body can be
Until something unthought-of occurs
And takes loved ones to eternity.

We forget how precious is each soul
And that life isn't always within our control
Hours, seconds or minutes...whatever the amount,
We must do our best to make them all count.

So dear ones remember and consider it true
That your life is precious and not just to you.
And countrymen, family and friends everywhere
Remember our nation and keep us in prayer.

?

We forget sometimes that
The entire world
Is connected as if by a thread.
And every time a tragedy hits
It is as if the whole world has bled.

Our Soldiers Are Heroes

Little Prayer for Our Heroes

May God bless you each and every one
For all you do for us each day
We will keep you in our hearts
And for your safety we will pray.

We know that you have left your homes
And your families as you answer duty's call
You have made an awesome sacrifice
And you are heroes, one and all.

Remember that no matter who you are
Or where you might be today
God hears and answers our prayers
As for your health and safety we all pray.

You are not alone on foreign soil
You have not been sent out to fail
For God knows and loves you every one
And with His help we will prevail!

?

May God bless you each and every one
For all you do for us each day
We will keep you in our hearts
And for your safety we will pray.

273

We Have Not Changed Enough

On that September day
Only one year ago
Harshest of reality
Dealt us an awful blow.

For a moment families drew nearer
And realized as never before
That loved ones were even dearer
And they loved them even more.

Citizens huddled together
On that awful day
And little children stopped to look
And could not bear to play.

Country clung to country
And united against one foe
Each one wanted to offer help
To keep freedom's torch aglow.

But through the months that followed
Evil men in our country carried out
Horrendous acts against our children
The worst things we could read about.

People continue to rob and steal
And hurt each other as before
Where is that unity of love
From the day we went to war?

Does patriotism only show it's face
When we are covered with ashes and dust
Can't we understand that every day
Being compassionate is a must?

274

Traitors still sell secrets
Over the internet
And perverts still email little kids
That they have never met.

Did we really change at all
On that fateful day?
Are our hearts any different?
What would the Father say?

Parents, teach your children
The difference between right and wrong
Teach them about the love and trust
That in a family belongs.

Children, look to your parents
As the ones who love you best
Love them and honor them
And by God you will be blessed.

Look around dear friends
And see if you agree
Do you see the changes
That we would love to see?

For if we have changed at all
We have not changed enough
For change is not really change
If displayed only when the going gets tough!

Oh Lord, we ask you to bless our land
And make us from now on to be
A land worthy to be blessed by You
As the land of the brave and free!
In Remembrance of September 11, 2001

When Daddy's Gone

Daddy, when you are gone out to sea
Our house is much too quiet for me.
And we don't laugh as much during the day
At the funny things people say.

We don't giggle so much out loud
But we do try to make you proud
By helping Mom and being good
Just the way you said we should.

When you are gone on deployment
It takes away from our enjoyment
Of anything that we love to do
For Daddy we are incomplete...without you.

We try hard to be so very brave
And every email we all save
And every photo, every word
And telephone message that we heard.

I store it all within my heart
The whole time that we're apart
And when you get back home again
My heart will wear a great big grin!

When you are gone on deployment
It takes away from our enjoyment
Of anything that we love to do
For Daddy we are incomplete...
without you.

I'll Be Brave

I will be brave, Daddy
When you have to deploy
Although it is so awful
And takes away my joy.

I will be brave for mommy
For she will miss you so
I love you so very much
Do you really have to go?

I will do my very best
To be good while you're away
I will be brave, Daddy
But... just not today!

You Are Not Alone

When you feel alone and blue
And discouragement rears its ugly head
In your heart's eyes picture this
Your little one praying for you
Kneeling down by their bed....

?

I will be brave, Daddy
But... just not today!

Letter from Daddy

My daddy loves me very much
And although he had to go away
He writes to us and thinks of us
Each and every day.

He told me the day he left
That he would hold me in his heart
And even though he's not at home
In spirit we are not far apart.

He said his love would stay with me
And to mind my mommy too
So that she won't have to be all stressed
Because she misses Daddy too!

Daddy wrote me a letter
One of my very own
It's been hugged and kissed
And to everyone it has been shown.

It may seem silly to some folks
That with my letter I won't part
But to me that letter is like holding
The love from Daddy's heart!

Daddy wrote me a letter
One of my very own
It's been hugged and kissed
And to everyone it has been shown.

God Bless the Soldier

God bless the soldier
As he goes to war each day.
Let him feel your presence
And send your peace his way.

We cannot begin to thank him
For all the brave deeds he will do
We have not the words to say...
That's why we are asking you.

We humbly accept the work he does
Knowing that it is a hero's life
Putting his duty and his nation
Before self, children and wife.

Oh Father, bless the soldier's wife
And let her know we care
And each time we feel that nudge from You
We will remember both of them in prayer.

You Have Our Back

'Tis said that you have our back
And will strive to do your part
While your protect our backs
We will keep you in our hearts!

Oh Father, Bless the Soldier's Wife...

Protector of Our Freedom

You are the protector of our freedom
And when you are far away from home
Know that our thoughts are with you
If you are feeling all alone.

Some of you may never have seen your child
Before you left for this awful fray
You may be new to this soldier's uniform
And it may be the first time you've gone away.

You may be right out of school
Or called out of your established daily life
You may have left your mom and dad
Or your husband or your wife.

You are involved in horrible war
Against the evilest of men
And all who know and love you
Pray that you will soon be home again!

But you keep on going
In a war that's just begun
Vowing not to come home
Until the war is won.

'Tis said that you have our back
And will strive to do your part
While your protect our backs
We will keep you in our hearts!

We will keep you in our hearts!

In Honor of YOU!

Welcome home soldier·
You are a hero in this town
That's why there are a lot of ribbons—-
Yellow ribbons-scattered all around.

It matters not how you arrive here,
If you come by train or sea or air,
You will see them at each station, dock or depot
You will find them everywhere!

These ribbons helped to remind us
While you were gone away
That you were fighting for us
And that for your safety we should pray.

They remind us of the families
That claim you as daughter or son
And that you are precious to them
Yes, each and every one!

They are bright like the sunlight
And float gently in the breeze
Held tight by doors and lampposts
And by both fat or skinny trees!

Welcome home soldier
You are a hero in our town
People here will be shouting welcome back
Before your feet can touch our ground!

Welcome Home Soldier

Faces of Bravery

On the news I saw heroic faces today
Faces of bravery the newscaster would say
As he mentioned each brave soldier who gave their life
And behind each of these is a
Mother, father, husband or wife.

Mothers' arms will feel an awful emptiness
And wives or husbands will miss their embrace
And little children will never again
Reach up to touch their parent's face.

Faces of bravery are still among those
Who fight in a battle they never chose
But who were willing to answer their country's call
Some gave a lot, but some gave their all...

Faces of bravery are also among us here
Trying their best their families to cheer
Trying to keep their heartache from showing
And trying to keep their loved ones from knowing...

Trying to keep loved ones from feeling their pain
From the feeling of not being able to go on again
Trying so hard to be brave for the daughter or son
Who won't see a mom or dad until the war is won...

Faces of bravery are evident in the schools
Teachers realize that little ones aren't easy to fool.
Little children keep on going as they walk out the door
Going to school as they did before...

Among the faces of bravery is the face of a wife
Who knows her husband daily risks his life
And a mother's brave face as she realizes too
Just what it is her child must do...

So many versions of faces of bravery
I see them so many places and it's true
I see a face of bravery in those
Loved ones who wait at home
I see a face of bravery in you.

The Sound of Freedom

Listen my son to the sound of freedom!
Look, my child, and see it pass.
Breathe in deeply the air of liberty
Pray each day for it to last!

There are those who would seek to destroy it--
The freedom that we love today.
Pledge my child that you will be vigilant
And on guard that we stay free.

For there is a price for freedom
And a cost involved in liberty.
Men have bought with their lives our freedom
Freedom never has been free!

Written July 4, 2001

A Soldier Farewell

It is so hard to watch you leave
But I know that you must go
I hold your hand and my heart aches
Because I love you so!

Although I hurt and ache inside
And the pain just will not end
I send you off with pride
And eagerly await the day
That you come home again.

I will think of you every day
And in the evenings when all is quiet
I will hold you in my heart
To dream about through the night.

Be strong and be safe my love
And I pray daily that you will be
Soon able to leave that awful battleground
To return safely home to me.

?

I will think of you every day
And in the evenings when all is quiet
I will hold you in my heart
To dream about through the night.

Protectors of Freedom

He is the protector of our freedom
And he is far away from home.
He may be very young
And may feel so alone...

He may never have seen his child
And his wife may be fighting too
Both of them may be in uniform
Defending the country for you.

He may be right out of school
And may have barely begun to shave
But he's out there in the fray
Our freedom trying to save.

He is involved in a horrible war
Against the evilest of men
And all those who know and love him
Pray that he will soon be home again.

But he keeps on going
In a war that's just begun
Vowing not to come home
Until the war is won.

'Tis said that he has our back
And will strive to do his part
While he protects our backs
Let's keep him in our hearts!

He may be very young
And may feel so alone...

Broken Hearted But Not Broken In Spirit

We will weep
Then we will mourn
For all that were lost
On that September day
When so many we loved
And who loved us
Were so hatefully taken away.

But even as we mourn
Together we begin to rise
First on shaking trembling knee
Then growing stronger
As one big American family
We will stand!

United is our cry
And united we shall be
Caring, sharing and rebuilding
This great big family!

We will not be stopped by hatred
Or give in to petty fights
We will not blame each other
Or step on each other's civil rights!

We will heal and we will recover
But we will never forget this day!
We will go forward with determination
That the evil ones will pay!

We will not fall into the trap
That evil itself has set in place.
We will not falsely accuse
And cause our country any disgrace.

Help us God Almighty
To right this terrible wrong.
Let our ears once again hear laughter
And our hearts once more be filled with song.

And let thankful hearts rejoice once more
As we move forward from this day
But let this love of family and country
Never fade away!
In Remembrance of September 11, 2001

For New Citizen

Congratulations on your becoming
An official American citizen today
Although it may be just a formality
It was important to hear them say...

That you are now pledged to loyalty
To the freedom you embrace
As a member of the citizens of American
And any foes which we may face.

Your citizenship was not begun today
This was just the final part
For the desires for liberty and freedom
Were born inside your heart.

So enjoy and celebrate the day
As we celebrate with you.
May your days be long and happy
And all your dreams come true.

Congratulations on your becoming
An official American citizen today!

A Question

What kind of citizens
Would the citizens be
If all of the citizens
Were just like me?

What kind of neighbors
And what kind of friends?
What kind of politicians?
The question never ends...

What kind of person
Is the right neighbor for you?
What kind of things
Do you want citizens to do?

What kind of message
Does your behavior send
As parents, neighbor,
citizen or friend?

?

Oh Father,
Bless the soldier's mother
And let her know we care
And everytime we feel
that nudge from You
We will remember both of
them in prayer.

Hug Us A Little Tighter, Lord

Hug us a little tighter, Lord
Hold us close today
We know that You are with us
And hear us when we pray.

Hold us a little closer, Lord
And let us feel Your presence near
We know that You see us
And see each and every tear!

Let us feel Your presence, Lord
In a new and special way
We know that You are with us
And won't ever go away!

Let us know Your power, Lord
Continue to lead and guide us
We know that we must follow
Your still small voice inside us!

Show us to how to help each other
And how to pass your love along
Hug us a little tighter Lord
Help us to be strong!

Hug us a little tighter, Lord
Hold us close today
We know that You are with us
And hear us when we pray.

Will We Smile Again?

This has been an awful month
With tragic reminders everywhere.
The only comfort comes
When we stop to say a prayer.

We want to laugh and smile again
And enjoy life each day.
But there is a sadness in our hearts
That just won't go away!

Children weep for martyred fathers
And mothers mourn for those who fell
The numbers of lives lost in this atrocity
Only time will tell.

Other countries too have suffered
With their sons and daughters lost
What is the price of liberty?
What is freedom's cost?

Where are the laughing children
That were schooled right down the street
From the once world famous towers
Where are those skipping feet?

Where are the happy couples
That walked there hand in hand?
Where once were tall proud buildings
Lies now a pile of sand.

Television newsmen
With cameras on their shoulder
Bring news about the madman
Who has made his henchmen bolder.

Pilots fly their airplanes
With the joy drained away
From a job they used to love
Until that fateful day.

Our country's heart is broken
And you can still hear us weep
But though that heart is hurting...
It hasn't missed a beat!

With God's help we will recover
Only He can heal our land
Only He can heal our hurting heart
And make us strong enough to stand.

In Remembrance of September 11, 2001

The Lady in the Harbor

The lady in the harbor still stands
A symbol of freedom
With her torch in her hand.
Still standing tall and straight
In the harbor of our hurting land.
Still welcoming those by air and sea
Who are seeking freedom and liberty.
Even if the terrorist bomb
Or plane used as a missile as before
Should seek her as it's target
We could only love her more.
Countless millions have stood in awe
With tear stained cheeks and hands on heart
And rejoiced as she came into view
A symbol of a brand new start!

Written September 14, 2001

A Man Is Never Taller

The tallest man I ever saw
Was bent over to help a child.
Lord, bless the man who is not too proud
To stop in the middle of the crowd
And help a little one
Someone else's daughter or son...

I believe the Lord above
Must be overwhelmed with love
When He sees a man
Kind enough to kneel
To mend a kid's bike
Or fix a scooter's wheel.

There must be a special place
In God's Heaven above
For men who show the Father's love
And share with children who ask
How to do some kind of task.

God bless the man who is not too tall
To bend to help the smallest of us all.
Lord bless the man, young or old
Who never lets his heart grow too cold
to bend to help a child.

God bless the man who is not too tall
To bend to help the smallest of us all.

292

Celebrating Our Independence Day

Happy Birthday...USA

Today I saw flags waving
And heard the people shout
About their love for the USA
And that's what it's all about!

In almost every hand I saw a flag
Of red and white and blue
And on the young and old alike
Were worn those colors too!

Young babies had flags on their bibs
And mom and Dad wore tees
That said, "We love the USA!"
And ribbons waved from trees!

Fireworks filled the nighttime sky
With firecrackers popping loudly
As everyone smiled and celebrated
Their love of our country proudly!

?

Today is my country's birthday
I think I'll bake a cake
And put a bunch of candles on it
So that we can celebrate!

On Being Free

I can walk down the sidewalk
And talk to everyone I meet
I can say hello to politicians
Or cops out on their beat!

I can say the Pledge of Allegiance
I can sing Amazing Grace
I can say things about our President
(Could say it to his face!)

I can write without being censored
I can quote the Golden Rule
I can send my child to learn
At a private school!

I can do all of these things
And others besides
For in the home of the free
My family resides!

?

Look around you and enjoy
The freedom of this place
Enjoy the happiness
And the smiles on each face.

Look around you and proclaim
This is a lovely place to be
In the good ole USA
Home of the Brave and Free!

Watching the Fireworks

We sat in silence in the darkness
Waiting for the grand fireworks to start
They were advertised as being awesome
They were classified as works of art!

There would be bursts of awesome glory
With flaming arrows and shooting stars
There would be oohs and ahhs with each presentation
And without hesitation, spontaneous applause...

I confess I missed the fireworks
For something sweeter caught my eye
Than the show that was above me--
Those shooting stars up in the sky...

For through it all I watched in fascination
As though transfixed through time and space
For nothing in that sky show could thrill me
Like the precious looks of wonder on your face!

?

We love to watch the fireworks
And find in them delight
For they remind us
Of Freedom's lovely light.

We love to hear the noise they make
As they explode high in the air
Popping as they fall to the ground
Scattering remnants everywhere.

A Freedom Poem

Stop for just a moment
And take a look around
Listen to the voice of freedom
What an awesome sound!

I hear it in the silence
I see it in each face
Oh how glorious is our freedom
Let us revel in it's embrace!

I hear in the noise
Of the city's roar
I hear it in the mountains
And I feel it on the shore!

Oh what an awesome feeling
To be strong and brave and free
And know that every morning
We awake in Liberty!

Let us not take it for granted
Or treat it with disdain
Let us treasure our country
And bring honor to it's name!

Let us never let the enemy
Destroy what we hold dear
Let us never be overtaken
By complacency or fear!

Oh what an awesome feeling
To be strong and brave and free...

Our Flag (Olympic Flag)

As our flag came on the field
So battered, torn and proud
There seemed to be no tear free eyes
In that Olympic crowd.

I saw not only that battered flag
But those fallen so brave and good,
And watched as our fighting men and women
Far away from their homelands stood!

I could not help it – I rose to my feet
Alone by my TV
But I know in my heart of hearts
A country stood with me!

In Gratitude

Our thanks we give to our heroes
Who serve our country each day.
Our heartfelt appreciation we offer
For all they do and say.

Our appreciation is sincere
For we know that we should be
Offering prayers of gratitude
To those who help keep us free.

They do not all win medals
Or make the evening news at ten.
They serve their country every day
And you call them your friend.

Across the Harbor

Today I looked across the harbor
And was so pleased to see
That the view was still the same
That meant so much to me.

It has been almost two years
Since the fateful day
When the skyline of New York
Was so suddenly blown away.

So I vowed not to take for granted
When I chanced to see
Something of beauty and importance
That means so much to me.

Whether I'm out walking
Or in a bus or car downtown
I will treasure each opportunity
To take a good look around.

And I will take a moment
To appreciate what I see
And give thanks to my Creator
For the beauty He provides for me.

In Remembrance of September 11, 2001

It has been almost two years
Since the fateful day...

All Over the World

All over the world people are saddened
And hearts are broken as loved ones say farewell
When will our dear loved ones be home again?
We know that only time will tell.

All over the world people are crying
Weeping for those we know and love
And shedding tears of gratitude
For those who now reside with God above.

All over the world people are praying
Praying for your daughter, husband, wife or son
Holding up your arms when your strength fails you
Just like in Bible times was done.

All over the world people are praying
Praying for you when you are finally able to sleep
For the Father in Heaven knows what your need is
And Jesus, the Good Shepherd looks out for all His sheep.

God did not promise there would be no heartache
That everything would always go the way we think it should
But God did promise to get us through it all
And that with Him all things will work together for the good.

So keep your faith and look up toward Heaven
Trusting to the Lord to see you though
And know that people all over the world are praying
For every soldier, every parent, every loved one such as you.

All over the world people are praying...

When Duty Calls

I miss you so very much
Each and every day
I feel so sad to know
That you are so far away.

Although the miles that separate us
Seem insurmountable at times
No amount of miles on earth
Can separate your heart from mine.

I do not know when you can return
For duty must be fulfilled by an honorable man
And I will be strong and brave
Though sometimes it is hard to stand.

But the things that sustain me
And will get me through
Are the gentle loving memories in my heart
Each time I think of you.

For that closeness that we felt together
Will not leave now that we are apart
For it is not a matter of miles that creates love
But love is a matter of the heart.

Although the miles that separate us
Seem insurmountable at times
No amount of miles on earth
Can separate your heart from mine.

Olympic Torch

Arrival of the Torch

We watched in awe
As you came in to view
Oh, how the symbolic nature of you
Gave fuel to the immense pride
That each heart held deep inside.

So much has happened in our past
So much heartache that cannot be mended
But through it all we held fast
With patriotism that has never ended.

That is why we watch in awe
With tears in our eyes again
Scores and medals mattered not
Or the games that we might win.

We have won already with freedom's light
We have won with victory's song
We have won with liberty
So let the torch be carried on!

?

We watched in awe
As you came in to view
Oh, how the symbolic nature of you...

PETS

People all over the world love their pets, they consider them the equivalent of fur or feathered family and treat them with love and affection. Here in the USA, we are probably the most enamored with our pets and do everything we can to prolong their lives and fill their days with love and tender care.

We are able to talk with total strangers about our pets and form a bond with them as we sit in at the vet's or at the dentist's office because most people speak "pet" and most have had one type of pet or another at one time in their life.

Anytime you see a person with a new puppy you will see a long line of folks wanting to say hello and pet the furry little head. Here are a few verses for those special friends of ours.

No Pets

Mom and Dad said no pets
And they meant it, I could tell
But then we went out shopping
At a mall I know so well.

It started at the window
Of my favorite puppy store
And before the night was over
We were pet free no more!

All Pets

You can cuddle with your kitty cat
Or play chase the ball with your dog,
Feed your gerbils in their cage
Or pet your croaking frog.

You can hiss right back at your garter snake
Or chirp back to your tweety bird,
Make mooing sounds to a newborn calf
Or dress your ferret in a manner absurd!

But no matter what kind of pet you have
This one thing will ring true
Whatever the pet that you call your own—
That is most beloved pet in the world to you!

?

I had a friend that loved me
No matter what the day
Didn't matter what I did
Or what words he heard me say.

Didn't have to explain
If I was feeling blue
This friend of mine
My temperament always knew!

Loss of Pet

Some Tributes to Special Friends

There is something about the loss of a pet
That bonds both friends and strangers
In a very special way.
For anyone who has loved a pet
Will have kind words to say.

No one can be untouched by love
Given so unconditionally and sweetly
For when you love a precious pet
He loves you back completely!

Friends

We did everything together
From the time we were just 'pups'
You were the tiny furry one
And I was your two-legged friend.
I never realized that our togetherness
Would someday have to end.

I look back with no regrets
Over the things we did together
We were true blue loyal friends
In sunshine or stormy weather.

Only one regret I had then
And forever will
I regret my precious furry friend
That you are not living still!

Many years have come and gone
And new memories have been made
But still there are sweet thoughts of you and me
Playing outside in sun or shade.

We played hide and seek
And chase the ball
And catch me if you can
And you were my spy dog
To help me find the other kids
When we played "kick the can."

No other dog can ever replace
The friend I had in you
Because I learned about your kind of love
I've had other 'friends' follow you.

I've loved them all in a special way
And each one is so unique
I've learned to listen to their hearts
And can almost hear them speak.

And all of this love that has come to me
I owe to you my first furry friend
For having you first in my young years
Made me treasure each loving pet
That God would send.

No other dog can ever replace
The friend I had in you...

A Love Note From Your Kitty

People think that cats can't smile
But we can and often do
Every time you smile at us
Our hearts smile back at you!

People don't know that cats can love
But our kitty love is true
Whenever you speak to us with love
Our love goes back to you!

And for those folks that wonder
If there is a special place
Like the Heaven that you speak of
That human kind will grace...

Well God created you and me
And in His Master plan
I have to think He would include
One who is a loyal friend to man!

So don't worry about me dear humans
Cause I'm happy as can be
To have lived my life so filled
With the love you showered on me!

And when you get to Heaven
After you enter in the gate
You will see me on a cushion silky soft
As I purr contentedly and wait.

If there's a separate Heaven
Where kitty's go and stay
Just know that I'll be happy there
Where I can run again and play!

306

A Love Letter from Your Dog

People think that dogs can't smile
But we can and often do
Every time you smile at us
Our hearts smile back at you!
People don't know that dogs can love
But our doggie love is true
whenever you speak to us with love
Our love goes back to you!
And for those folks that wonder
If there is a special place
Like the Heaven that you speak of
That human kind will grace...
Well God created you and me
And in His Master plan
I have to think He would include
One who is best friend to man!
So don't worry about me dear humans
Cause I'm happy as can be
To have lived my life so filled
With the love you showered on me!
And when you get to Heaven
After you enter in the gate
You will see me bring my favorite toy
And I will wag my tail and wait.
If there's a separate Heaven
Where doggies go and stay
Just know that I'll be happy there
Where I can run again and play!

Love, Your Doggie
as told to Thena Smith

I'm So Glad I Kissed You Goodnight

We found you by accident
A tiny bit of cuddly fur
And we were so overjoyed
At what a precious pup you were!

I had never kissed a puppy dog
And never on its head
And I had always said with conviction
"There will be no pup on my bed!"

We brought you home with us
While the day was sunny and bright
And played with you so happily
Until the day turned into night.

We put you in your tiny bed
And you didn't want us to leave
We couldn't stand to see you cry
And our hearts began to grieve.

We held you close and cuddled you
Until you ceased to weep
Then we kissed you on your furry head
And watched you go to sleep.

Through the years you blessed us so
And brought us immense delight
Until one morning we found you still
When came the morning's light.

I thought of the hours just before
When you and I had been up late
We had cuddled on the sofa and watched TV
Our mommy-doggie date.

I had carried you to your little bed
And in it placed you lovingly
Thankful for the fun we'd had
And all you meant to me.

I said sweet loving things to you
And before I left your bed
I bent over your sweet doggie form
And gently kissed you on your head.

As I looked at your sweet still form
My eyes teared unrelentlessly at the sight
And I whispered to your tiny frame
"I'm so glad that I kissed you goodnight."

I do not know if God's Heaven holds
Dear pets that we love so
But if there is such a place
It's where you are, I know.

And I pray that angels knew you by name
When you came into sight
And that they play with you all day
And then kiss you goodnight.

I had never kissed a puppy dog
And never on its head
And I had always said with conviction
"There will be no pup on my bed!"

My Doggie

God gave us this dear pet to love
And we took this task to heart.
We always treasured this dear dog
Cherished him from the very start!

We know that sometime he will leave
And though we will cry and we will grieve
In our hearts and minds will stay
The cherished memories of every day!

We would not want for him a life of pain
Just for a few more months to gain
But if leaving us is in God's will
Though he may leave we will love him still!

For I truly believe that in God's plan
Is also room for these friends to man.
I know that somewhere He has a place
Where (Bear) can find a ball to chase.

So thank you Father up above
For giving this dog to us to love
And for each day we have him here
To hug and love our (pet) so dear!

Charmy

True friendship is hard to find
And with his I was blessed
For truly this friendship was mine
In the form of my dog Charmy!

I Miss You

I miss your happy wagging tail...
Your bark and yes, your smile
I will not forget you my dear friend
You've been family for quite a while!

Some may scoff that I might grieve
And may not understand my pain
But my heart will not completely heal
Until I see you again!

For surely the Creator
Who gave you to us to love
Has pet accommodations waiting
In His Heaven up above!

My Rat Pal

Once I had a special pet
Who had a long and skinny tail
I kept him in a little cage
And feed him from a pail.

He didn't chase a ball
And didn't purr like a cat
But he was the top of the line
As far as being a first class rat!

I miss his little pointy nose
I miss his little tail
My eyes tear up each time
That I see his empty pail.

My Good Friend

A good friend is hard to find
Especially as wonderful
As this friend of mine!

He was a loving loyal friend
With love that seemed to know no end.
All too soon his life was gone
But memories of him will linger on.

I know I'll see him again someday
When my life is o'er
For I have heard that God's Heaven
Has a doggie door!

?

Giving and Caring

Always giving
And always sharing.
You loved me faithfully
Beginning to end
Proof of the proverb
That you are man's best friend.

Hardshell Pets, Feathered Friends and Other Much Loved Pals

Turtle Verses

I took this photo of a turtle
And I know so very well
That turtles are exciting
With a wonderful story to tell.

But it is hard to get enthusiastic
And do something artsy and unique
When you have lots of turtle photos
That show no head or feet!

The turtle can be picky
And when you have your camera aimed
He can go inside his big ole shell
And play a waiting game!

Just when you put your camera away
Out pops the turtle head and feet
He's played this game for years and years
And is very hard to beat!!

I took this photo of a turtle
And I know so very well
That turtles are exciting
With a wonderful story to tell.

Look at the Turtle

Look at the turtle
So old a creature is he
At home on land
Or at home in the sea.

They are so determined
And so very wise
With a shell to protect them
And keep the sun out of their eyes.

Other creatures may die out
And become rare or extinct
But not the turtle
He will survive I think!

A Great Story

I love the story
Of the tortoise
And the hare
Although some rabbit fans
Claim the race unfair.

They say all manner
Of things to save face
But we know that
Slow and steady
Can really win a race!!

I love the story
Of the tortoise
And the hare...

You Can't Hug A Frog...

Some people like all kinds of pets
From dogs and cats to mice
But as for the perfect pet for me...
I think frogs are nice!

Frogs are very easy to please
And like to live in a stream
Frogs are always very nice--
I've never seen a frog that's mean!

People hug their cats and
They cuddle with their dogs
Now you can hold one in your hand
But you can't hug a frog!

Nope! You really cannot hug a frog
And this is not a joke...
You can't hug a frog
Or it might
cr·oak...

I was so excited
When Mommy said
That she had a frog in her throat
But I never ever saw it
She should have made sure
Before she spoke!

Yes, I'm a Parrot

Yes, I'm a parrot
And my name isn't Polly
I don't sing show tunes
Like "Hello Dolly."

I don't want a cracker
So don't ask me if I do
But if you speak nicely to me
I might say, "hello," to you!!

Little Lady Bird

My name is not Tweety Pie
And I don't like baby talk
If I were a parrot
It would make me squawk!

My name is much more formal
Than those most generally heard
For I am quite the genteel parakeet—
I'm a dainty ladybird!

?

Mothers see them as slithery creatures
With no cuddly warmth or
Cute fuzzy features...
As slimy and creepy
With a tail that won't end
But boys see a snake as a wiggly friend!

Dogs And Cats

Dog Gone Cletus!

Carmen's sweetie had a doggie
Cletus was his name
But things are sad at Carmen's house
Cletus is in shame!

Cletus felt a need for comfort
In the middle of the night
And knew that if he snuggled up
That would be all right...

So up jumped Cletus onto the bed
And made himself at home
Well Carmen tossed his buns right out--
As if he were a bone!

It made Cletus very sad
That he was not wanted there
He needed to find a shoe to chew...
Ah he spied a pair.

His instincts got the best of him
And before Carmen could intercede...
Cletus lifted up his leg...
And on her shoes... he peed...

Carmen's sweetie had a doggie
Cletus was his name...

Being a Puppy

Being a puppy brings with it a lot of uncertainty. Sure, we are cute and cuddly and people stop and look at us, but so many of them just want to oh and ah and play for a moment, but don't really want the responsibility and commitment that comes with taking one of us home. I had been in a tiny cage for a few days and while it was fun being there with my little sister, I knew that eventually one of us would leave. (I had watched some of my puppy friends go out the door with strangers and I wondered how they could leave so happily with people that they didn't even know!) Then you and Melissa came in and picked me up and talked to me and cuddled me....and I knew.... I just knew! Then you said, "Your name is Cozy and I'm your new mommy. You are going home with me! Would you like that?" "Oh, yes!" is what I wanted to say, but all I could do was wag my tale until I thought it would fall off! You and Melissa took me to your new house and I knew that I had found my home with you!

Write the story of how your fur babies joined your family from their perspective. It gives you such a close feeling to them when you try to put yourself in their place.

Dog Bath

I'm a tough cookie
I don't need this pampering.
Rubbing and scrubbing
Cause severe spirit dampening!
Just when I feel like
I know who I am
I feel hands pulling and tugging
And I'm in the bath...bam!
My name is Bandit
I'm rough and tumble.
If you try to bathe me
I'm just gonna grumble!
I don't like baths.
I don't mind saying,
And once you are finished
In the dirt I'll be playin'!

Doggie Kisses

Great Gramma has a doggie
Kiley is it's name
She likes to hand out kisses
And is so very tame.
She kissed me on my nose
And before I knew what to do
I had another kiss
And it was a wet one too!
Not that I mind the kisses
It just took me by surprise
And I got some of her kissy stuff
On my face and in my eyes!!

319

Everyone Needs A Pup

Everyone should have a pup
To love and hug and cuddle up!
A little bit of fur and fluff
Of this you just can't have enough!

Everyone needs a pup to train
But from yelling, please refrain
For a pup will pee and poop and chew
And try the patience out of you!

But just when you are about to break
His little puppy head he'll shake
And give a little puppy bark
That can melt the coldest heart!

And then he will come to lick your face
While held tightly in your loving embrace
For one of the best things puppies do
Is show you how much they love you!

Even once your puppy is grown
And able to do things on his own
He needs your love and training too
So he can be a best friend to you.

And though he may weigh much more
And have longer legs than at the start
Inside the largest dogs of all
Seems to beat a puppy heart!

Everyone should have a pup
To love and hug and cuddle up!

Playmates

Gustauf (Gus) and Cozette (Cozy)
are the best of friends.
They play together every day.
I know they chat an awful lot
Though I'm not sure what they say.
Gustauf is white with curly hair
And has a boyish frame
While Cozette is very feminine
Black with a long, straight and silky mane.
They get along so very well
And every toy is a special thing.
Both of them love music
And each one loves to sing!
They have such fun together
But like siblings everywhere
Sometimes they get a bit cranky
At the things they have to share.
They love to be together
And they know we love them so
That's why they don't understand
That some places they can't go.
They sit so sadly by the door
As I go to work each day
And can't understand at all
Why I can't stay home and play.
But though I'm not their actual mommy
I take very seriously
The task of guardian to Gus and Cozy
For these puppies are special to me!

They play together every day...

Cat-i-tude

My cat has an attitude--
I call it a cat-i-tude.
He shows not one bit of gratitude
For his daily pampered life!

I know it may be a platitude
To discuss cats and their attitudes
But just a hint of gratitude
Would be a welcome sight!

I know a cat is very smart
And carries goodness in his heart
And I've known it from the very start
They are superior pets!

To my cat it does not occur
That he could give a gentle purr
When I stroke and brush his fur
As "thank you" for this care?

Or a gentle kiss upon the cheek
A loving game of hide and seek
"I love you," said in "Kitty Speak"
Is that too much to ask?

But will it happen??
I think not.
I will be content
With what I've got!

My cat has an attitude--
I call it a Cat-i-tude!

Owning a Cat

Let me tell you that...
You can never OWN a cat!
You may offer a cat a home
But he reserves the right
To be owned!

A cat, if invited right
May concede to spend the night
In your abode or residence
But being owned will not make sense.

A cat will be a haughty friend
And mixed messages may send—
One moment inviting loving pats
Then leaving without a backward glance!

A cat will turn up his nose
At the very food he chose
And go instead to someone next door
Who offers something he likes more.

And if you head for your best chair
You can bet that he'll be there
Snoozing and purring and looking so sweet
That you head for another seat.

Somedays cats can be a lot of fun
And on others they act like brats
But we put up with it all
Because we love our cats!

Let me tell you that...
You can never OWN a cat!

More on Cats!

Cats are really a lot of fun
But there are some things they do
They make us kinda crazy
For a moment or two!

For instance when you have work to do
Is when your cat wants attention from you
And you can say move or scram or shoo
But a cat just demands more of you!

And reading the paper is the call
For the cat to bat the ball
Right onto the part you are reading
And for sure some cuddling he'll be needing!

And when it's time to go to bed
Watch out where you lay your head
Cause on the blanket or on your pillow
You will find your furry little fellow!

And in the night onto your bed he'll climb
And take up so much of the space
That you will have to hug the edge
Or the railing of the bed embrace!

And why we let the kitty sleep
And worry about them waking
When all the while it is Our Bed
And OUR space they're taking!!

It all boils down to this I guess
No matter what we say
A cat is a cat is a cat
And we love our cats this way!

When Meeting a Cat

I should tell you
When meeting a cat
Don't panic or fret
Don't worry... well, not yet...
A cat upon first meeting
Might seem rather haughty,
Perhaps a bit stuck up
And even rather naughty.
She may turn up her nose
And stiffen up her back
Causing you to fear
That she might attack.
She may remind you
Of creatures of long ago...
Her royal ancestors
And she would prefer it so.
From the lioness
So strong and brave
That one could never caress
Comes this attitude, I would guess!
But once she has the chance
To check you out
And get good feelings in her mind
A loving creature you will find.
She may still be stubborn and haughty
And at times a bit lazy perhaps
A pet inclined to prefer your best spread
For her dainty little cat naps.
But she will become part of the family
That you can't do without
For that is what being owned by a cat
Is all about!

POEMS OF LOSS

Friends rejoice with each other and celebrate joyous occasions together, but the test of a true friend is how they help you through the tough times, the sad times, the times of heartache and loss. A friend who sticks close to you when you need them the most is a treasure indeed.

Loss is so hard for all of us to deal with. Especially difficult is the loss of a child and unfortunately, I have been called on several times this year to write poems for grieving parents or have had parents tell me that they used one I had posted on a site for someone else.

I hope none of you need these verses but it is my prayer that your reading them will fill your heart with even more compassion for those about you who grieve.

Here are the feelings
From deep in my heart
Words from my soul
That I long to impart.
Words of love so heartfelt
That I long to share
Some read like poetry
...others a prayer...

Loss of Baby

Nestled in God's Arms

The Lord loves little ones
And keeps them safe and warm
In a special place in Heaven
Nestled in His arms.

The Lord placed the tiny babes
To grow in a mother's womb
And if He calls them home before their birth
He must have them a special room.

I have not yet seen Heaven
But I know our God above
Will take special care of tiny ones
And surround them with His love.

So do not fret or mourn
For the tiny soul set free
But look forward to a reunion
That will last eternally.

?

The Lord loves little ones
And keeps them safe and warm
In a special place in Heaven
Nestled in His arms.

Dedicated to Baby Mason

Is there anything sweeter than a newborn baby
So fresh from the heart of God above
To fill a home with happiness
And fill parents' hearts with love?
As parents to be, we waited in such joyous anticipation
Planning all the things that new parents plan
And doing all the things expectant parents do
Happily looking forward to the day when we
Would be holding you.
Your grandparents walked around with beaming faces
Filled with joy that soon they would welcome you
And teach you such wonderful things
about life's mysteries
And do all the wonderful things grandparents do.
But your time upon this earth was all too fleeting
And you came but briefly as I heard the angels sing
And it must have been your guardian angel
That gently brushed my falling teardrops with her wing.
And as quickly as the earth below had welcomed
And held you in loving hands and heart
God reached down with gentle hands from Heaven
And with our precious Mason we had to part.
We love you our dearest little Mason
And we know that you are safe and dearly loved
Enveloped in the loving arms of Jesus
In a beautiful mansion up in Heaven above.
Though we may weep and show some sorrow
And some might say, "Sometimes life's just not fair."
In our heart of hearts and in our inner spirit
We know that you are where you are safest
Nestled sweetly in the arms of Jesus
Now and forever in the Father's care.

328

So Very Quietly You Came

So very quietly you came into our lives
But it was much to early for you to come to stay
And so we were left with empty arms
And hurting hearts
As just as quietly you went away.

So sweetly you came into this world
Not asking for anything save air to breathe
And just as sweetly you drew that last breath
And with tear filled eyes
We wept as we watched you leave.

So gently we held you in our arms
For such a little while
Trying to memorize your tiny face
And that precious little smile.

The time we were allowed to hold you in our arms
Was so very sweet but oh so very short
But God above created our minds in such a way
That we can forever hold you in our hearts.

*Written in loving memory of Mason
who ever so quietly slipped into God's arms
after only a few brief moments on earth.*

So gently we held you in our arms
For such a little while
Trying to memorize your tiny face
And that precious little smile.

Our Little Love

How lovely were those few sweet days
And oh, so bittersweet
When I held you near my heart
Thinking soon my world would be complete.

Complete it would be with baby things
And cuddly snuggly toys
Filled with tiny talcum smells
And newborn baby noise.

We never got to hold you in our arms
Before we had to part
But for those few short blessed weeks
We had held you in our hearts.

We will see you someday little one
And we will hold you then
Our family once more will be complete
And the circle of our love will never end.

?

Even though you miss them terribly
This child loved so much by you
May you find your comfort in
How much the Father loved them too.

Bittersweet Day

The days that we had planned for
And longed for
And thought would make our lives complete
Were gentle days and precious days
But oh, so bittersweet.

Each second became a treasure
And each hour was held tightly to our hearts
And each sweet day was so precious
That we did not know how we could bear to part.

But God in Heaven reached down to touch
The little one we love so much
And though we knew he must go away
We knew that there's a spot in each heart
Where he will always and forever stay.

I do not fault my God of love
For I know He wished my babe no harm
And God felt the safest place for him to be
Was in his Father's arms.

Baby Cap...Loss of Child

I hold your little cap to my face
And in my heart, it is you I embrace
For in this cap is your sweet baby smell
The one I love and know so well.
I know you are in the Father's care now
And that you will forever stay
As a precious little fragrance
To Heaven's sweetest bouquet.

What If...

I was pondering today
The words a tiny babe might say
If they were taken from the earth
Very close to their moment of birth.

What if they could look here below
And send us a love note to let us know
That they were happy and content
And that their time was not misspent...

"Mommy and Daddy just want you to know
That I realize you love me so
And that you didn't want me to leave
But please don't cry and fret or grieve.

God meant no harm to you or me
But my problems He could see
And knew that in Jesus arms
Was the best place for me to be.

An angel came and brought me here
And Mommy and Daddy she saw your tears
And even though she did not speak
With her wing she brushed your cheek...

I live in a lovely mansion here
With such a wonderful view
It has a rocking chair and crib
And there's a special room for you!

I know that you won't be here
For a very long long time
But just wanted you to know
That your room is next to mine!

I hope you enjoy your life on earth
And don't worry about me at all
For I have so many friends
And angels on whom I can call!

Sometimes we go outside
And the clouds are rolling by
And I know that you are looking up
And see them in the sky!

When you look up on starry nights
And see them so bright and clear
Just know that they are not nearly as lovely
As they look from here!

I love it here and I'm so happy
That Jesus loves me so
And He loves you just as much––
Just wanted you to know!

Well, I must go back now
But remember if you will
That I loved you while in your arms
And I love you still!

Take care dear Mommy and Daddy
And love your lives for me
For I know that our time together
Was so much shorter than
You thought it would be!

Do not rush your life to get here
For I don't mind the wait
And my face will be the first you see
When you enter the Pearly Gates!"

To My Child

They say not to fret and cry
That I will have another baby
Another child to take your place
But that child won't have your face...

That child may be beautiful and smart
And have a special place in my heart
But it will never fill that part
That was yours alone.

They say not to mourn and cry any more
That life has so much in store
And I should stop my fretting
And get about the business of forgetting...

I will be strong and go on living
I will be loving, caring and forgiving.
But never in a million years
Even though I'll dry my tears...
Will I stop loving you!

You will always be in my heart
Always and forever a special part.
And when I walk inside Heaven's gate
I'll look for you where loved ones wait!

You will always be in my heart
Always and forever a special part...

Loss of Loved Ones

Years From Now

When people turn the pages
Of this lovely book about you
There is one thing I would ask—
One thing I would have them do.

I would ask that they search their memories
And remember you, the man
The husband, father, grandfather and friend
And try to understand.

You were never just a page
Flat and one dimensional in a book.
You were life and love and joy
In every breath you took!

Your friendship was coveted
And treasured by all those who knew
The outstanding man you were
Each day your whole life through.

This book is made in memory
Of a life you lived so well
And even after we too are gone
Your story it will tell.

This book is made in memory
Of a life you lived so well
And even after we too are gone
Your story it will tell.

To My True Love

Do you remember (how could you forget)
The time and the way in which we met?
It only took one look for me
To know that my life's love and soul mate
You were destined to be.
Do you think it was fate
Or perhaps the Lord above
That brought us together
And let us fall in love?
Sweetheart, you were my life.
You were my treasure
And making you happy
Was my greatest pleasure.
I loved sharing with you my life
I loved the joy of having you as my wife.
I adored the way that you looked at me
And the gentle touches on my hand or knee.
You always knew just the thing to do
To make me happiest our whole lives through
And the only thing that I would have wished for
Is to have spent with you a hundred years more.
You touched my heart in such a special way
You knew just what I was going to say
It was if we were two halves that made a whole
With a love that filled my heart with joy
and touched my soul!
God knew that you and I
Shared a love that would never die
And even though the time seemed short to me
He was fitting us to be together forever
In His Eternity....

In Loving Memory

Sometimes God sends an angel
To earth in human form
To shower us with kindness
And make our souls feel warm.

With compassion love and understanding
And a heart molded from His above.
God sends an angel to live with us
To fill our days with love.

Don't ask me how I know this
But I'm sure that it is true
For there is no other explanation
For a blessing such as you!!

We lay you to rest with aching hearts
But hearts filled with peace and love.
Knowing that you are now with God
And seated in the heavenlies above.

For if God allows an open window
For loved ones to watch us from above
We know that you will watch over us
And all of those you so dearly loved.

You were loved as mom, grandmother,
great grandmother and friend.
And as each one a special treasure
To be you will always be in our hearts
Loved beyond all measure.

You filled our days with love...

Did You Know

Did you know I loved you
And how much I cared?
Did you realize how I treasured
Those moments that we shared?
Did the time move slowly for you
When we were out of touch
I hope you knew I loved you
So very, very much.
I know that I can not go back
To good times of years ago
But in my heart I love you still
And I pray that this you know.
If you can look down from Heaven
And see the love within my heart
Then you know I shall love you always
Even though we had to part.

A Christmas Prayer for You

Sometimes our lives bring things
Which we don't understand
And it is difficult to see
Just where was the Master's Hand.

But God will work all things out
If we just give Him the chance to do
The things He knows are the best
And then He will see us through.

So my Christmas prayer for you
Is that God above would bless
Your life, your day your very being
With His peace, joy, love and happiness!

For You My Love

For you my darling I have so much love
And so many tender feelings in my heart
I have shed so many tears each day
Since God called you away
And we were forced to part.

But in my heart are treasured memories
Of kinder and happier times
Times when first united in love
Were two hearts-yours and mine
And with those memories I shed tears
As I reflect and remember those precious times.

I pray that God welcomed you with arms open wide
And said, "Yes, this is Heaven...
Won't you please come inside
Without that earthly body to weigh upon you
There is nothing here to get you down
We have your room ready and waiting
And have prepared your crown."

Don't worry about us darling
Just keep watch for us at Heaven's gate
And when we get there, whenever God calls us
We will look for you where loved ones wait.

Don't worry about us darling
Just keep watch for us at Heaven's gate...

The White Rose

Each Mother's Day my grandmother would go to her rose garden and bring back beautiful roses for all of us to wear to church. She would give my mom, my brothers and me each a red rose and she would always chose a beautiful white one for herself.

One day I asked her why we wore red roses and she wore a white rose. "You get to wear red because your precious mother is living," she explained, "and I wear white in memory of my dear mother."

That was the first time I realized just how special Mother's Day was. Far too few years passed before my mother wore a white rose on Mother's Day. Through out the years we wore a rose to church and I was swept back in memory to my grandmother's garden and the smell of her roses as she pinned them on our Sunday clothes.

...And all too soon I had to exchange my red rose for one of white and how I treasure the sweet memories of my red rose years.

Sometimes God sends an angel
To earth in human form
To shower us with kindness
And make our souls feel warm.

God Bless Those Who Hurt

God bless those at Christmas time
Whose hearts are in such pain
That they lack the energy to go on
And just want the hurt to end.

Let us not be so self- involved
That we would turn away
Lacking the very spirit
Born on that first Christmas Day.

Let us reach out to those in need
Whether from pain or lack of funds
To share the true meaning
Of Christmas with everyone!

And let our love so bless them
That they will feel anew
The joy of that first Christmas
And the blessed Gift from You!

?

I see so many people
Whose hearts are full of sadness
And they can't celebrate today
For they own no gladness.

Father, please brush away their tears
And fill their hearts anew
With a wonderful Christmas joy
That comes directly, Lord, from You.

God Did Not Promise...

God did not promise that nothing
would grieve us
But He promised instead that He would
never leave us...
God did not promise that we would
have no fears
But He promised to be there to
brush away tears...

God did not promise that there would be
no high water
But He promised to stay with each
son and each daughter...
God did not promise we would never
leave earthly friends
But He promised that in Heaven life would
have no end.

He did not make us puppets and He will not
pull our strings
We are only earth bound creatures until Heaven
gives us wings!
He says that when we need Him,
He is always there
He is never very far away...
He is just
as close as a prayer!

God Did Not Promise...

Mom Went Home For Christmas

Mom went home for Christmas
She knew it all along.
"I'll be home for Christmas"
She sang it like a song...

Mom went home for Christmas
She smiled and left us there.
We knew it was her heart's desire
We knew it was her prayer.

Mom went home for Christmas
And though we miss her here,
I know that she is happy now
And I feel that she is near.

Mom went home for Christmas
And I know she couldn't wait
And I know that she will welcome me someday
When I get to Heaven's gate.

I Know She is There

I take comfort in the fact
That I know my mom is there
I take comfort in the knowledge
I find comfort in my prayers.
I find solace in the Scriptures
And knowing God's Word is true
And knowing she trusted Jesus
With each breath her whole life through!

Mom Went to Sleep Tonight

Mom went to sleep tonight on earth
For the very last time
Leaving her earthly body with its precious smile
And a loving little sigh
The spirit of my precious mom
Winged its way up to the sky.

She was my best friend, my confidant,
the heart of my life
She was a mother, grandmother, a daughter and a wife
Who lived for her family and did amazing things,
Whose smile could light up a room and
cause the saddest heart to sing.

She loved my dad and he loved her for a lifetime of years
And her leaving this earthly plane will cause
him many tears.
They were never without each other and
never wanted to be apart.
They were a two people but they shared one loving heart.

Mom loved us and we each knew that she did
We had no doubt of this
For she showed us every day
In her every action and in every way
and with each hug and kiss.

Mom loved to play her games with friends
And did for quite a while.
Her place at their table will be empty
And they will miss her loving smile.

I know that her many friends and loved ones
Who have gone to Heaven before her
Were standing at the place where loved ones wait
Smiling and waiting for her.

How happy they must have been to see her
And how thrilled my dearest one
Must have been to enter into those Pearly Gates
And embrace the one she called her son.

I do not know if Heaven has windows
And loved ones can look down here to see
The families and dear ones left behind
Before they come to share eternity.

But I know that Mom's love is all around me
And I know that I can face each new day
By knowing she is in Heaven
And I will join her there some day!

Mom went to sleep on earth tonight
And left this earthly sod
Only to awake in Heaven's wonder
And to finally see the face of God.

*Written for my friend Donna upon
the loss of her dear Mother*

She was My Best Friend,
My Confidant,
the Heart of My Life...

Mom, I Miss You

Mom, I'm being selfish now
Because of how much I miss you--
But I wish you were still here with us
And that I could hug and kiss you!

I know that you're in Heaven now
Seated at Jesus' knee.
But sometimes I ache so awfully bad
For you to be here with me!

It was so hard to watch you leave
And, Mom, I must admit
There's grief and hurt inside of me
That I'm not over yet.

I cried so hard and wept so much
That I could not speak or see--
Until I felt His touch upon my head--
And heard, "YOUR MOTHER IS WITH ME!"

?

Mom went to sleep on earth tonight
And left this earthly sod
Only to awake in Heaven's Glory
To finally see the face of God.

Heart Song

My heart has a voice
That it uses to sing
It knows the words
Of love songs and things...

It knows the words
To songs of friends
It knows songs of blessings
Without any end...

But sometimes in times
Of hurt and distress
My heart forgets the song
That it once knew the best...

And in those trying times
Lord, I turn in faith to You
And ask You to restore my song
And let my heart sing anew.

?

Prayer for Peace

Father please grant me your peace
Please, let me be accepting
And put my mind at ease.

For I am really hurting now
And it seems it will never end
As I mourn the loss of not only my Mom
But my best and dearest friend.

347

My Mother's Hands

My Mother had such lovely hands
Whose touch comforted me for years
Wiped away fever from my brow
And my many childish tears.

My Mother had such gentle hands
Whose touch I remember every day
I can still feel her tender touch
Though she has gone away.

But though I cannot hold her hands
Nor feel them on my brow
I know exactly where they are...
The Father holds them now...

We Grieve With You

We grieve with you
Because you grieve
And although it won't make
the sadness leave
I hope that it will comfort you
To know your friends are grieving too!
We hurt with you
Because you hurt
And because we love you so.
It won't make the pain go away
But we wanted you to know.
And when you dry your saddest tears
And your heart begins to mend
We will all rejoice to see
Your happy smile again!

Remembering

I rejoice for you today
Even though you've gone away.
For you start your eternal life
Reuniting with your husband
Who waits for his beloved wife.

I will not weep that you are gone
For I shall greet you before too long.
And then you can show me the Heavenly sights
Where your star shines bold and bright.

I rejoice now that you are free
As God intended you to be
I weep not, because I know
That someday your face I'll see.

So look for me as I approach
And I will smile as I get near
For you are still in my heart and mind
As someone precious and very dear.

The rainbow that I saw today
Looked beautiful to my earthly eyes.
But I can only wonder now
How the view looks from paradise.

Look down on me once in awhile
And know each hug I give or get
Has lingering thoughts of your dear face
And in my heart, I hug you yet.

I rejoice for you today...

Take Time To Grieve

Take time to grieve
And yes, to weep
But cherish sweet memories
For those you will keep.

Do not forget
Though it now makes you sad
For someday remembering
Will again make you glad.

We know that sorrow
Never entirely goes away
But the burden will grow lighter
And you live from day to day.

Rejoice in the time
That you had to love
And look forward to reunion someday
In Heaven above.

For God knows every heartache
And He sees every tear
And the one that you love so much
The Father also holds dear.

Remembrances

Here are my remembrances
Of life long friends
And of love that knows no distance
And will not end.
Here are sweet mementoes of times long past
Of friendships that will last and last.
I store these memories here in part
The rest is stored within my heart.

Remembering Loved Ones

Sitting with my album
Looking at the past
Remembering my loved ones
And when I saw them last.

Time is slowly healing
The pain once oh so sharp
And has filled with sweetest memories
That hole left in my heart.

I miss them all so very much
But I think of them and smile
And I know that I shall see them again
Though it may be awhile.

In God's Word, I find my comfort—
It's as if I hold His hand
And I know that when in Heaven we're reunited
Then I will understand.

Would I wish them back again
As mortals here below?
If God would ask me if I would
My answer would be "no".

For though it may be painful
To miss them as I do,
My greatest comfort Lord
Is in knowing they're with You!

Remembering my loved ones
And when I saw them last...

Time Will Heal Your Hurts

Time will slowly heal
The pain, which is now so sharp
And will fill with sweetest memories
That hole left in you heart.

Think of the one you miss
Think loving thoughts and smile
And know that you see him again
Though it may be awhile.

In God's Word find your comfort
It's as if He holds your hand
And know that when in Heaven
You are reunited
You will understand.

For though it may be painful
To miss him as you do
Let the knowledge that
He is with the Father
Bring peace and comfort to you.

Your Time

Your time should have been much longer
Upon this earthly sod
But I am comforted in the knowledge
That you are now at home with God.

In God's Word find your comfort
It's as if He holds your hand...

Remembering You

I sit and look at your photos
And photos of the two of us.
We really didn't take enough...
Neither of us really liked a fuss.

But today each one is priceless,
A treasure with worth untold.
I would not part with one of them
Not for a bundle of purest gold.

For I can still gaze upon your face
And in doing so in my mind I can hear
The wonderful and melodious sound
Of your voice which was so dear.

You were more than just a friend
You were a person so unique,
A person who listened with your heart
To every word that I would speak.

I will never forget you, dear one,
And the friendship that was ours
And with our happiest of memories
I have spent so many pensive hours.

Our time should have been much longer
Upon this earthly sod
But I am comforted in the knowledge
That you are now at home with God.

A person who listened with your heart
To every word that I would speak...

Poem of Loss

Thank you Father God above
For all those you gave to us to love
And for all of those who love us too
Dear Heavenly Father...we THANK You!

You sometimes hear us cry and fret
And complain that we weren't ready yet
To watch those whom we love leave
And you comfort us as we cry and grieve.

Sometimes we think we can't bear the pain
And that we won't ever smile again
But then You send someone our way
To help heal our hurts and brighten our day.

We all have lost loved ones this year
One of our dear friends that we met here
But Lord in our hearts we know it's true
That they are all so much better off with You.

?

Sometimes it seems the Father
Calls home too early those we love
And brings them safely to his throne
In Heaven up above.

And though you miss them terribly
This child loved so much by you
May you find your comfort in
How much the Father loved them too.

Our Grandmother

She was always a sweetheart
And always such a dear
With a heart that just grew sweeter
With every passing year.

She had a charm about her
That when she entered into a room
She chased away all shadows
And any hint of gloom.

She was loved by all who knew her
And right from the very start
Every member of her family
Knew she was its very heart!

Never did a cross word
Come from her lips as such
And those who cherished her
Treasured her loving and gentle touch.

I know Heaven will be sweeter
To have our Grandmother within it's Pearly Gates
And I know that when we arrive there
We will be wrapped in her embrace!

She had a charm about her
That when she entered into a room
She chased away all shadows
And any hint of gloom.

355

SPECIAL NEEDS

Sometimes we are faced with difficulties and trials.
It is particularly difficult when our beloved children are involved. But we must keep in mind that God doesn't make mistakes and so many times people are blessed beyond their wildest expectations by what originally was a disappointment.

When our children are born with physical or mental difficulties our original plans must be changed and a new plan put into effect. It doesn't mean it is a lesser plan, just a different plan.

I have a friend whose first little boy was born with Downs Syndrome and as I visited the nursery in the hospital when he was born, instead of the happy and excited mommy and daddy I had expected, the mood was very quiet and sad. The doctor had just told them the news and they were shaken.

Suddenly their hopes, dreams and goals for this young one had to change and they had to be very practical about just what he could and could not do. The first matter of concern was his health and after that they would have years of getting the best mental and physical training for him that they could find.

God healed the hole in this little baby's heart that could have shortened his life, and placed in that little heart one of the sweetest natures on this earth. He is a teenager now, but I can still feel his toddler arms around my neck. He used to pull my face close to his to see me better and then his eyes would light up as he said, "Thena!" My eyes would always light up when I saw him as well.
I love you Colin!

Yes I See Myself in You

Yes, I see myself in you
I can also feel your heart.
I feel that you are part of me
A very special part!

Do not worry or weep
About the way I seem to you.
For I know that God loves me
And I am special too.

There are such sweet things inside my heart
And I know God placed them there
Special and wonderful things
That I don't know how to share.

I do not envy a single good thing
That God has given you
For I know inside this heart of mine
That He has blessed me too.

?

I believe that in God's plan
He searched the whole earth through
To find the perfect parents for this child
And decided to bless you.

Our Love for You

We listened as the doctor told us that you had "problems"
And we had no idea what that would mean to us or you.
We only knew that we had wanted you
And waited for you and loved you.

We listened to what well meaning folks said when
They saw you and how they sympathized with us
That you were not "well."
We only knew that we had brought you
Home and needed you to be with us
And that we loved you!

We are so grateful to our friends who share our
Love for you and who never say how sad that your
Health will never be quite right...
We only knew that God in Heaven
Created you and sent you to us
And loves you
And you are perfect in His sight.

Special Needs

God has blessed our family
With a bundle from above
One that needed
Our special kind of love.

Though to the human eye
Some things may not seem right
It is such a blessing to know
That he is perfect in God's sight!

I See in You

I see pure joy in you every day
As you go about your sweet unassuming way.
Seeking naught but to love us
Such a precious angel you are
You are one in a million
Our tiny little shinning star.

You light up the room with your presence
And chase away any fear or doubt
You hold in your loving acceptance
The meaning to what life is all about.

Unwavering in your loyalty and devotion
You hold out your hands to touch each face
That holds for you a special meaning
And then wrap your arms around us in sweet embrace.

You have taught me more
Than you could ever know
As I watch you live and love and grow
And because of your pure and tender heart
At the end of my life's journey
I shall be a better person
Than I was at my journey's start.

You are one in a million
Our tiny little shinning star!

Grandchild (Downs)

Child of my child
Child of my heart
I love every inch of you
Each precious part.
With a face like an angel
And skin soft to the touch
I kiss you and cuddle you
And I love you so much!

They call you a Downs Child
And some say, "Oh, how sad."
But to have been without you
Would have been sadder than sad.
I cannot imagine my world
No matter how I try to
Without my sweet grandchild
To love as I do.

How I love to feel your tiny hands
Sweetly caressing my face
And see the light in your eyes
As we snuggle and embrace.
And each time I see you
My heart takes a leap
In thanks for a miracle
So perfectly unique!

And I thank the Father
For sending such a delight
My grandchild, so wonderful,
And so perfect in His sight.

Your Child, God's Blessing

I watched you as your nursed your newborn son
And snuggled him close to you.
He was not the "perfect" child you planned
What had God given you?

Where was the child that you dreamed of?
And what would happen to your dreams for him?
How does God choose the child for parents
That He would send to them?

Perhaps God looked into your heart
And saw something good and true
And knew that his beloved treasure
Would be safe with you.

We teach our children daily
All the things they need to know
But sometimes it takes a special child
To help us really grow.

A special child can teach us so much
And God counts them Jewels In His plan
And only when you've been blessed by one
Can you begin to understand.

I believe that in God's plan
He searched the whole earth through
To find the perfect parents for this child
And decided to bless you.

Perhaps God looked into your heart
And saw something good and true...

You Are Special

My dear child you are so special to me
Always have been, and always will be!
When you hurt, I hurt too
And nothing can change my love for you!

I love you more and more each day
No matter what you do or say.
And although sometimes you make me sad
Having you for my son makes my heart glad.

You will always be my most valuable treasure
And my love for you is beyond measure.
You are my love, my hope my joy
My wonderful and much loved little boy!

No one on earth could take your place
And I pour my heart into our every embrace.
Knowing that you hurt sometime...
Makes my love more fierce dear child of mine.

My prayer for you will daily be
That God above will let you see
Just how very precious
You are to me!

Everything done by God's hand is perfect
And every action He performs is right.
His hand created you and He sent you
to us for us to love you and you
are an object of His delight!

My Darling Said, "I Love You"

My darling said, "I Love You"
And the words caused my heart to leap
Although they weren't the first words
That I heard my little one speak.

Each sentence is a struggle
And each success a victory
That's why it is so special
That he said these words to me.

Soon they will be more natural
And easier for him to say
But they will never sound any sweeter
Than they did today!

Sweet Child of Mine

Sweet Child of Mine
I want you to know
That my greatest delight
Is to watch you grow!

Sweet child of mine
My love for you
Is something that nothing
On earth can undo.

Sweet child of mine
Be you one or 99
You will always be my baby
Sweet child of mine.

There is a Future

There is a future for you
Perhaps different than you had planned
For God never lets you stumble
Without holding to your hand.
You may feel that life has wronged you
Or that God has let you down
But He knows your every tear drop
And sees your every frown.
Keep looking to the future
And hold on to your faith
Don't let depression scar you
And take you out of the race.
I cannot promise what the future holds
Nor what the ultimate plan may be
But I know who holds the future
And I know who holds the key.

Hold My Hand, Mommy

Hold my hand, Mommy
It shows me that you are nearby
Sometimes I just need to feel your touch
And so I fret or cry.

Touch me when you can, Mommy
My face or arm or hair
It just reminds me of your presence
And lets me know that you are there.

Kiss my cheek, Mommy
Run your fingers over my face
Hug me tight, Mommy.
I thrive in your embrace.

Today I Said, "I Love You"

Today I said, "I love you."
And it made my mommy smile
I've never said the words before
But I've thought them for quite awhile.

Today I said, "I love you."
And every word came out
It made me feel so happy
I wanted to clap my hands and shout.

Today I said, "I love you."
And it gave her such delight
That Mommy pulled me close to her
And hugged me oh so tight.

I know the words are special
And I've wanted for so long
To say them to my Mommy
For in my heart they are my song.

I hope my Mommy knows how much
I mean those words I finally said
And I hope I will repeat them again
Tonight when I'm snuggled in my bed.

I hope that when she tucks me in
And before she turns out the light
I will be able to say them once again...
...Please God, let the words come out right!

Today I said, "I Love You"
And it made My Mommy Smile...

The Words in My Heart...

The words in my mind are clear as day
But when I try to say them to you
There may be a bit of delay
And you may not understand the words that I say.

The words on my lips are formed perfectly
And I know exactly what I want them to be
So don't judge me unkindly or think I don't know
What I want to say if my wording is slow.

The words in my heart are plain as can be
I wish that everyone who knows me could see
And hear them as clearly as I
The words in my heart as speak them I try.

God hears my words and He gave them to me
And when I pray to Him, I speak perfectly
For He sees in my heart each word I say
And understands perfectly each prayer I pray.

My Hero

I'm always so proud of you
But especially so today.
I know that it wasn't easy
But you were a brave soldier all the way!

You faced each doctor and each nurse
All the technicians and even worse
With such a wonderful attitude
That my heart was bursting in gratitude.

This day will soon just be a memory
In a long list of your days that will be
But in this heart of mine, it is the day
That you became a hero to me!

A Prayer for My Special Child

Father, it is to You I humbly come
To thank You for my little one.
To others he may seem to have defects odd
But I realize that he is a gift from God.

If only part of this little one
Could be a replica of God's Son
I would not choose that outer part
But pray instead for a perfect heart.

I thank You for this special treasure
That You have sent our way
And ask that around this little one
You station Your guardian angels every day.

I know that he may have some trials
And many struggles to overcome
But I trust in You Dear God
To carry him through each one.

I confess that this is not the baby I pictured
That perfect baby that I had in my mind
But I will not worry or try to second guess
The hand of the Divine.

So I lift him up to You Dear Lord
And ask that every day
You touch and bless and comfort
For it is in Jesus' Name I pray.
Amen

Father, it is to You I humbly come
To Thank You for My Little One.

Someday We Will Be Whole

For those who have no sight on earth
Who had not this gift of sight at birth
Just think about how wonderful it will be
When Heaven is the first sight they see!

For those who on earth are colorblind
Just picture the Heavenly colors divine
And think how wonderfully they will be blest
When on those colors their eyes will rest...

For those who have no legs to walk
No arms to reach
No speech to talk
Just think about the wonder of
Running and talking in Heaven above!

I do not count these gifts as trite
The gifts of arms or gifts of sight
But I value more than words can tell
Knowing that in Heaven I someday will dwell.

And when I approach the Heavenly gate
And look around at those who for me wait
I will not see one missing limb
We'll all be perfect when we see Him!

And when I approach
the Heavenly gate
And look around at
those who for me wait...

Twins

We are twins
It's plain to see
I see myself in you
Do you see yourself in me?

I will be the hand you need
For things you cannot reach.
I will be your teacher
For the things I'm able to teach.

You will teach me patience
And inner strength and compassion
And perhaps I shall teach you
Of humor, fun and fashion.

I love you as I love myself
And promise you to be
The part of your wonderful self
That you physically cannot be.

Twins

God created us twins
And though some folks would say
That we are different from each other
I do not see it that way!

You are like my other self
And I can almost read your thoughts today.
You would love to run and jump
And sing and laugh and play.

When I do the things
That you are not able to do
I do them not just for me
But I do them for you too.

TEDDY BEARS AND OTHER MUCH LOVED FRIENDS

One of the most universal objects of affection is the teddy bear. I have frequently been called upon by someone wanting to document this affection on a page, a plaque or for a framed and decorated wall hanging. Teddy bears are recognized by young and old alike for the loveable stuffed friends they are.

People of larger size who are kind and dear to us are often referred to as teddy bears. We love their hugs and we tend to snuggle close to them for their warm embraces. (I am becoming rather "teddy bearish" myself!)

As I finished the last chapter in this book, I realized that I had not included my fun fur, cloth or fabric friends and felt that they must be included. Fortunately, there was just enough room left—although one might say "bearly" enough!

Once I had a teddy bear
Who seemed so real to me
That I was sure his button eyes
Could really truly see!

Teddy Bear

Once I had a teddy bear
Who seemed so real to me
That I was sure his button eyes
Could really truly see!

For many the years this once fine bear
Through the ravages of time did go
Until his button eyes fell off
And his seams began to show.

But I loved him just as much
As I did when he was new
And though it may seem silly--
I know he loved me too!

For he was always smiling
Though his fur began to thin
And when I was sad or lonely
I could expect his teddy grin!

There's something special about teddy bears
They are awful brave and smart
And if you ever looked inside--
I'm sure you'd find a heart.
12/8/85

There's Something Special About Teddy Bears...

An Ordinary Bear

I'm just an ordinary bear
But I'm never put away.
For when people see me
They always want to play.

Through the years I've met them all
Kids and grownups too
Who need the love a bear can give
For a teddy bear is true.

A teddy bear is loyal
You can wear his fur right down
From loving him and hugging him
And he won't even frown.

I've had my share of roughies
Who toss me in the air
And pull my legs and pinch me
And pull my teddy fur.

Then there are the older kids
Who pretend that they don't care
But secretly deep inside of them
They want a teddy bear.

A teddy bear is kind
A teddy bear is true.
If you want a special friend
A teddy bear's for you!

So treat your bear with kindness
And love him every day--
'Cause teddy beers are sensitive
In a very special way.

Even when our eyes are gone
And our limbs are ripped part
You find our love is just the same
If you look inside our heart.

Everyone Needs A Teddy Bear

Everyone needs a Teddy Bear
To hug when they are blue
Everyone needs their Teddy Bear
To hug the long night through.

Everyone needs a Teddy Bear
To hug when they are glad
And to shed hot tears upon
When the world makes them feel sad.

For a Teddy offers comforts
When you are sad and blue
Is there to snuggle when you need a friend
And asks nothing back from you.

So take good care of your Teddy Bear
And keep him warm and well repaired
And treasure all of those memories
Of the times the two of you have shared!
3/09/02

Everyone needs a Teddy Bear!

Teddy Dear (Bear)

Teddy is my dear stuffed bear
My favorite toy is he
Teddy is so dear to me
That I like to keep him near to me!

Teddy sleeps with me in my bed
Right up close next to my head.
He snuggles with me all night long
And when we vacation he comes along!

When I am happy, he is there
My fun and joy he loves to share!
And when I'm sick, lonely or sad
To hug him makes me feel so glad.

His hide is just is a little worn
But never has he been forlorn.
Teddy is such a well loved friend
Top to bottom and end to end!

He is so very brave and smart
With tons of love in his stuffed heart.
Oh Teddy dear, I love you so
And in your heart I think you know!

Teddy is my dear stuffed bear
My favorite toy is he
Teddy is so dear to me
That I like to keep him near to me!

Jangles

Jangles is my dear stuffed cow
My favorite toy and my best pal!
Jangles is so dear to me
And I like to keep him near to me!

Jangles sleeps with me in my bed
Right up close next to my head.
He snuggles with me all night long
And when we vacation he comes along!

When I am happy, he is too
And would say so if he could only moo!
And when I'm sick, lonely or sad
To hug him makes me feel so glad.

His hide is just is a little worn
But never has he been forlorn.
Jangles is such a well loved friend
Top to bottom and end to end!

He is so very brave and smart
With tons of love in his stuffed heart
Oh Jangles dear, how I love you
Even if you cannot "Moo"!

Jangles is my dear stuffed cow
My favorite toy and my best pal!
Jangles is so dear to me
And I like to keep him near to me!

My Blanket

My blanket is a special friend
That I just cannot let go
I know he's tattered, torn and ragged
But I love him so!

It's been with me so very long
That it's like a part of me
You would not ask me to give up
A finger or a knee!

Well, Blankey is a special part
I hug him close right to my heart
And if I feel a hint of fear
I hug my little blanket near.

Someday I know he will be all gone
I will have worn him way too thin
But as for now I hug him close
My raggedy blanket friend!

?

It's been with me so very long
That it's like a part of me
You would not ask me to give up
A finger or a knee!

Cuddly Wuddly

Cuddly Wuddly
Soft and sweet
My fuzzy lamb
With which I sleep.

If he were black
Or brown or blue
I would still
Love Lamby true.

When he gets tattered
Or ragged and torn
I'll love him still
Even if he is shorn.

Cuddly Wuddly
Is my favorite sheep
And through the night
He makes not a peep.

And when comes
The morning light
He is right beside me
Where he was last night!

Cuddly Wuddly
Soft and sweet
My fuzzy lamb
With which I sleep.

CONTRIBUTORS TO THIS BOOK

Ural Donohue ~ My thanks to my friend Ural for the use of her lovely poem. Ural has been writing poems for her family since she was a child. Her other hobbies are scrapbooking, bird watching, and genealogy. I met Ural at my first Scrapbooking club ...Leora's Scrapbooking Clubhouse on Yahoo and she has been a continual source of inspiration, encouragement and joy. Her love for people and for the Lord is evident in her every word and action. Thank you Ural for sharing and for being you!

Debbi Seiler ~ My thanks to my friend Debbi who is the founder of my first scrapbooking club, Leora's Scrapbooking Clubhouse. She is a nurturing mother hen to all of us and everyone is inspired by her thoughtfulness, gentleness, kindness and humor! Through this club I have met online and in person so many wonderful friends. Debbi (or Leora, as we call her) is a wonderful and dedicated wife, mother and grandmother and it is to the memory of her sweet grandbaby that some of the baby poems were dedicated. Thank you to Debbi for letting me share these very personal poems which I wrote for you, to comfort others.

Carrie Heissler (Weehoo) ~ Thanks to another member of The clubhouse for the cute version of my A Boy is A Joy poem. Carrie is the mother of two wonderful boys who bring joy to her home and heart but she is able to see the humor and truth in parenting situations. She is a constant source of joy in our lives! Her third "joyous" addition is due in November.

Merryann Phillips ~ I shared a poem that I wrote for Merryann's Dad's graduation. She is a source of great joy in my life. She is a talented artist who has overcome a lot of obstacles in the last few years but her faith and courage has been a blessing to all of us who know and love her.

Shirley Stoeckel ~ Shirley and I met when our girls were in grade school and have been the best of friends for 20 years or more even though now we live hundreds of miles apart. Shirley is one of the dearest and most genuinely sweet persons you will ever meet and very talented. She sings in a well known choir as well as writing poetry and songs. She has two wonderful daughters and two handsome son in laws along with three adorable (and perfect) grandkids! Shirley and I co-wrote a children's musical several years ago and produced it locally. It was one of the most fun and rewarding things I had ever done and she is a joy to work with. When I get to Heaven and God tells me that she was really an angel on earth....I will not be surprised!

Sharon Hammon ~Sharon is a wonderful Christian wife, mother and grandmother who has been so encouraging and inspiring since the first day we met about two years ago. She recognized me from the online article that I write for PCCraftter.com. She approached me at the San Diego Expo and we started talking ....and we haven't stopped yet. She was such a blessing in her proofing hundreds of poems for me even though she had plenty of other things to do. Sharon's home was recently endangered in the California wildfires of 2003, but thankfully, it was spared.

Linda LaTourelle ~This book has always been my dream and thanks to this wonderful lady, Linda LaTourelle, who is Bluegrass Publishing, it is becoming a reality. I cannot begin to express my gratitude to God for bringing us into each other's lives. We have adopted each other as sisters and plan on doing a lot of projects together. Linda lives in Mayfield, Ky and is the author of three "Ultimate" books, and I have had the honor of having verses included in two of them. She has more books to come, so be watching her website at www.theultimateword.com and your local scrapbook retailer.

CONTRIBUTORS CONT.

CC Milam ~ CC lives in Mayfield, Ky with her husband and two lovely daughters...with one more girl on the way! She has had a passion for poetry and writing since she was very young. She feels that it helps her capture a moment in time that can be remembered through words. She hopes that her writings help others to relate and feel peace, joy and comfort. These can only truly be experienced by knowing Jesus Christ as your personal Lord and Savior. Her prayer is that you will experience His abundant love and love overflowing grace. CC is a published author in "The Ultimate Guide to the Perfect Card" by Linda LaTourelle. CC took categories of my poetry and put together chapters to create this book. This is the second book that she has edited that has been published. She is my Editing Angel.

Todd Jones ~ Originally from Glasgow, Kentucky, Todd lives in east Tennessee with his wife Cindy. Together they homeschool their children Will, Olivia and Garrett (well, really Cindy does, but Dad helps). He expresses his artistic talent through graphic and structural design by day. At night, he moonlights as a wannabe bassist, playing a variety of music. In getting to know Todd, it is easy to sense his love for the Lord. He is an extremely talented man with great vision and insight, with a giving heart, too. A blessing indeed!

RECOGNITION

We are very grateful to Lettering Delights for being so kind to allow us to use their "LD Hand" font as the main typestyle in the book and their "LD PeekABoo" font. We think that this spiffy looking font adds the finishing touch. I want to say a very special thanks to everyone at the company! THANKS!

Lettering Delights...For AWESOME looking fonts that will make your layouts and other projects zing with creative genius, be sure to visit this wonderful website and stock up on the best fonts you'll find. It's a user friendly website, designed so that you can not only preview these great fonts, but you can download them immediately for a nominal fee. Or if you're a font addict like I am, you'll want to have them all on cd's for easy access. I have been using their font creations for years now and love how they're always coming up with fun, new fonts. They're a terrific company, with super customer service.

Also, every month they have contests and a chance to win free fonts. They've even got a freebie section and newsletter, too. So have a visit and expand your font horizons!

www.LetteringDelights.com

Need another book?

Are you looking at your friend's book right now?
Order your own copy below or go to our website at:
www.theultimateword.com
Send us an E-mail:
service@theultimateword.com

MAIL ORDER FORM

Please send _____ copy/s of:

Where's Thena? I need a poem about...

Name: _____

Address: _____

City: _____State_____Zip: _____

E-mail: _____Phone: _____

Please include $19.95 plus $2.95 s/h (per book)
(KY add 6% tax)

Bluegrass Publishing
PO Box 634
Mayfield, KY 42066
Tel. 270.251.3600

If you're looking for a gift that will be
treasured and used regularly... Order now!
Where's Thena? I need a poem about...
Available at your local scrapbook retailer, too.

FAVORTIE LINKS

Digital CD's and Downloadable Artwork

www.cottageartsnet.com
www.pcccrafter.com
www.esrappers.com
www.123scrapbooking.com

Clubs

www.leorascrapbookclubhouse.com
http://groups.msn.com/SunnroomScrappers

Magazines

www.simplescrapbooksmag.com
www.creatingkeepsakes.com
www.memorymakersmagazine.com
www.stampington.com/html/legracy.html
www.simplysentiments.com

Websites With Shopping Message Boards

www.scrapvillage.com
www.daughterswish.com
www.idreamofscrapbooking.com
www.pagesoftheheart.net
www.lifetimemoments.com
www.scrapjazz.com
www.onescrappysite.com
www.twopeasinabucket.com
http://mb.embellishedmemories.com

And For My Favorite Books

www.theultimateword.com

NOTES